D0515094

More Oral Sadism and the Vegetarian Personality

Readings From the Journal of Polymorphous Perversity®

Also by Glenn C. Ellenbogen, Ph.D.

Oral Sadism and the Vegetarian Personality: Readings From the Journal of Polymorphous Perversity®

The Primal Whimper: More Readings From the Journal of Polymorphous Perversity®

Freudulent Encounters for the Jung at Heart: Still More Readings From the Journal of Polymorphous Perversity®

The Directory of Humor Magazines and Humor Organizations in America and Canada

More Oral Sadism and the Vegetarian Personality

Readings From the Journal of Polymorphous Perversity®

Edited by
Glenn C. Ellenbogen, Ph.D.

NATIONAL UNIVERSITY
LIBRARY   SAN DIEGO

BRUNNER/MAZEL, *Publishers* • New York

Library of Congress Cataloging-in-Publication Data

More oral sadism and the vegetarian personality : readings from the Journal of polymorphous perversity / edited by Glenn C. Ellenbogen.
 p. cm.
 Includes bibliographical references and index.
 ISBN 0-87630-795-0 (pbk.)
 1. Psychology—Humor. 2. Psychiatry—Humor. I. Ellenbogen, Glenn C.
II. Journal of polymorphous perversity.
 [DNLM: 1. Psychiatry—humor. 2. Psychology—humor.]
PN6231.P785M67 1996
150'.207—dc20   96-783
                    CIP

Oral Sadism and the Vegetarian Personality
 Copyright © 1980, 1981, 1993 by Glenn C. Ellenbogen.

Curing a Phobia
 © by Art Buchwald. Reprinted by permission of the copyright holder.

Little Red Riding Hood
 Reprinted with the permission of Simon & Schuster, Inc., from *Politically Correct Bedtime Stories* by James Finn Garner. Copyright © 1994 by James Finn Garner.

New Horizons in Psychoanalysis: Treatment of Necrosistic Personality Disorders
 © 1986 by The University of Chicago Press. This is an abridged (by the editor) version of an article originally appearing in *Perspectives in Biology and Medicine, 29*(4), 493–498. Reprinted by permission of the copyright holder and author.

Just for the Health of It
 © 1993 by Richard Lederer. Excerpted by permission of the copyright holder from *More Anguished English,* published by Dell.

All other selections © 1992, 1993, 1994, 1995 by Wry-Bred Press, Inc.

The name *Journal of Polymorphous Perversity* is a Registered Trademark under exclusive license to Wry-Bred Press, Inc.

The material appearing in this book originally appeared in the *Journal of Polymorphous Perversity,*® a psychology humor magazine available by subscription from Wry-Bred Press, Inc., P.O. Box 1454, Madison Square Station, New York, NY 10159-1454.

More Oral Sadism and the Vegetarian Personality: Readings From the Journal of Polymorphous Perversity®
 © 1996 by Wry-Bred Press, Inc. All rights reserved.

All rights reserved. No part of this book may be reproduced by any process whatsoever without the written permission of the copyright owner.

Published by
BRUNNER/MAZEL, INC.
19 Union Square West
New York, New York 10003

Manufactured in the United States of America

10 9 8 7 6 5 4 3 2 1

To Ilene—my partner in laughter, love, and play

Contents

1 Psychodiagnostics

2 Psychotherapy

Preface

The study of human behavior is a serious matter, right? Fortunately, I've never seen it that way. Throughout my studies toward earning my doctorate in clinical psychology, I came across many situations that struck me as, well, funny. Take, for example, the incident that happened while I was on my three-month "rotation" through the psychiatric emergency room of Kings County Hospital during my one-year internship. A patient, waiting the typical four or five hours to be seen in the psychiatric E.R., complained to the triage nurse that he experienced everything as "foreign and strange." The reward for the wait was to finally be escorted into a small examination cubicle. There he was introduced to Dr. Gandhi, who was apparently unable to speak more than a few words of English (although the words "schizophrenic" and "manic depressive" seemed to roll right off his tongue). The patient told Dr. Gandhi that he perceived everything as foreign and strange. In fact, he even shared that he experienced *Dr. Gandhi* as foreign and strange. Dr. Gandhi, who had no appreciation of the concept that even a broken clock is correct at least twice a day, understood little, if anything, the patient was saying, and the patient was immediately carted off to the locked unit for treatment.

My clinical internship came in the last of my five years of doctoral training. I had managed to keep some semblance of sanity during the first four years of formal coursework—surrounded though I was by intensely earnest graduate students and somber graduate-school faculty—by writing spoofs of psychology, which were published in various magazines. In 1980, having successfully survived the oral defense of my doctoral dissertation—"the primal hump"—I was awarded my Ph.D., whereupon I promptly founded Wry-Bred Press, a small publishing company. Around the same time, I wrote a lampoon of the No. 1 intelligence test in use in psychology, calling my

IQ measure "The Scale of Mental Abilities Requiring Thinking Somewhat" (SMARTS). Wry-Bred Press published the piece as a free-standing "monograph," under the banner of a fictitious journal— the *Journal of Polymorphous Perversity*. Soon I began receiving letters of encouragement from mental health professionals, and, more important, humorous submissions to a journal that did not really exist. The message was clear: the field of psychology was in desperate need of some good laughs.

On January 2, 1984, the first issue of the *Journal of Polymorphous Perversity* was launched, with "Psychotherapy of the Dead" as its lead article. But I knew that it would be an uphill battle to successfully market this irreverent magazine. The American Psychoanalytic Association outright banned its display at the group's annual convention, declaring that humor was "inappropriate."

Eventually, however, more issues of the *Journal of Polymorphous Perversity* made their way into the field, and I started to see signs that the magazine was beginning to have an impact. Reprints of articles (such as "The Etiology and Treatment of Childhood") were creeping into college psychology textbooks. I began to receive invitations to present humorous talks before state and regional psychological associations. Finally, Brunner/Mazel, a leader in decidedly serious professional psychology texts, asked me to put together an anthology of *Journal* pieces.

In 1986, Brunner/Mazel published *Oral Sadism and the Vegetarian Personality,* taking a gamble on publishing its first humor book—and one that satirized its bread and butter to boot. To the publisher's relief, the book was enthusiastically received, becoming a bestseller, translated into both German and Japanese. A second anthology— *The Primal Whimper*—followed in 1989, with a third collection, *Freudulent Encounters for the Jung at Heart,* published in 1992.

Which brings us to 1996 and *More Oral Sadism and the Vegetarian Personality.* (The original article that started it all—"Oral Sadism and the Vegetarian Personality"—appears as the second piece in this wacky new collection of spoofs drawn from the pages of the *Journal of Polymorphous Perversity*.) Brunner/Mazel has once again made it possible for me to unleash a full frontal assault on the stuffy, the stodgy, the stoic, and the stolid. It's a tough job but . . .

New York, New York   Glenn C. Ellenbogen

Acknowledgments

I would like to gratefully acknowledge the help of the following *Journal of Polymorphous Perversity*® associate editors, who were kind enough to review manuscripts that touched upon their speciality areas:

Milton Spett, Ph.D. (Clinical Psychology), Edward E. Coons, Ph.D. (Comparative/Physiological Psychology), Gregory N. Reising, Ph.D. (Counseling Psychology), Les Halpert, Ph.D. (Developmental Psychology), George E. Rowland, Ph.D. (Engineering Psychology), Richard J. Koppenaal, Ph.D. (Experimental Psychology), James F. Harper, Ph.D. (Forensic Psychology), Robert Perloff, Ph.D. (Industrial Psychology), Gordon D. Wolf, Ph.D. (Medical Psychology), Charles F. Levinthal, Ph.D. (Neuropsychology), Chris Holle, M.S.N. (Psychiatric Nursing), Benjamin Strouse, M.S.W. (Psychiatric Social Work), Robert S. Hoffman, M.D. (Psychiatry and Neurology), Estelle Wade, Ph.D. (Psychoanalysis), Hilary James Liberty, Ph.D. (Statistics), David O. Herman, Ph.D. (Test and Measurements).

As the definition of what constitutes "good" humor is very subjective, the associate editors were rarely in agreement, either among themselves or with me, about which articles merited publication. The responsibility for making the final selections for the regular journal issues and for this anthology was ultimately mine and mine alone. The presence of any given article in this anthology should not be construed as reflecting the endorsement of the associate editors.

Finally, I would like to thank the many authors whose works appear in this anthology.

Photo by Tara Studios

GLENN C. ELLENBOGEN earned a BA and MA, both in Psychology, from New York University, and a second MA in Psychology from Hofstra University. Psychologically unable to cope with having MAMA after his name, he resolved his problem by earning a PhD in clinical psychology from Hofstra University.

Successfully surviving graduate school with some sanity intact, Dr. Ellenbogen founded the Wry-Bred Press and launched the *Journal of Polymorphous Perversity,* a humorous and satirical journal of psychology aimed at "injecting a dose of humorous medicine into the aging veins of psychology." Writing under his own name and such pseudonyms as Ernst von Krankman (literal translation from German meaning "seriously from a sick person"), Seymour Fruitlooper, and William Goodenough (reflecting his modest self perception that his writing was, well, good enough), Dr. Ellenbogen has written and published in the *Journal of Polymorphous Perversity* ground-breaking articles on such topics as oral sadism and the Vegetarian Personality, tactics for keeping one's shrink awake during the therapy session, and a new fragrance by Calvin Kline—Borderline.

More Oral Sadism and the Vegetarian Personality

Readings From the Journal of Polymorphous Perversity®

1
Psychodiagnostics

Psychometric Infallibility Realized: The One-Size-Fits-All Psychological Profile

David A. Levy, Ph.D.
Pepperdine University

Throughout the 20th century, reliability and validity have been the dual goals of psychological testing. Although these standards were adequate for the clinician of yesteryear, they have failed to keep pace with the ever-growing demands of modern society. As we stand at the threshold of the 21st century, the time has arrived for psychological testing to come of age by setting its sights on the third, and most important, psychometric property: interpretive infallibility.

Despite decades of painstaking research on countless batteries of psychological tests, we have scarcely begun to quench people's insatiable thirst for security in the belief that someone out there understands them better than they understand themselves. This simple but powerful principle—which astrologists, palm readers, psychics, cult leaders, and authors of self-help books have known (and capitalized on) for years—underlies the astonishing success of the consummate method of interpretive infallibility, the One-Size-Fits-All Psychological Profile (OSFAPP).

As its name denotes, the OSFAPP system has been shown to be equally effective for clients of all ages, vocations, races, cultures, religious backgrounds, sexual preferences, political affiliations, and presenting problems. Further, its results are guaranteed irrespective of the clinician's education, training, or experience. In fact, this system is especially useful to clinicians of limited intelligence.

However, the greatest strength of the OSFAPP lies in its atheoretical nature. Much like the latest installment of the *Diagnostic and*

3

Statistical Manual of Mental Disorders (APA, 1987), the OSFAPP can be used by clinicians of varying theoretical orientations, by clinicians with no theoretical orientation, and even by clinicians who are not quite sure what a theory is. For example, you are free to explain to your client that the results of the OSFAPP were based on a meticulous analysis of any one of a number of the client's offerings: dreams; free associations; stories about a series of out-of-date, black-and-white pictures; statements to an empty chair; drawings of people, houses, and trees; or favorite fairy tale, color, or television game show host. If none of these techniques appeals to you (or if you wish to add an extra touch of mystique to the process), simply inform the client that you drew upon your finely tuned powers of "clinical intuition."

Armed with the OSFAPP, the clinician of tomorrow will never again run the risk of being embarrassed by an incorrect test interpretation. Why settle for empirically derived, data-based, or scientifically validated interpretations—all of which are subject to error—when you now have it within your power to provide the client with irrefutable truths? At the very least, clients will feel that they have gotten their money's worth. At best, the OSFAPP method ensures a permanent place for psychological testing in clinical practice, sure to thrive and prosper well into the next century.

The One-Size-Fits-All Psychological Profile

Developmental History

You are the kind of person who was biologically conceived by two, opposite-sexed parents. However, no one, including your mother or father, ever asked you if you wanted to be born. For a period of time, you were totally dependent on others for food, shelter, and safety. Your vocabulary was extremely limited, you found it impossible to stand up without assistance, and you were incapable of doing even the most mundane of tasks, such as brushing your teeth. In fact, for awhile there, you didn't even *have* any. On more than one occasion, your cries went unheeded.

Things are different now. You are not as young as you were. You've had numerous experiences in your life. You've had some problems and suffered some disappointments. When things haven't worked out the way you intended them to, you wished that they had.

Physiological Processes

You're the type of person who has many and varied physical needs. For example, when deprived of oxygen, you are likely to experience feelings of suffocation. Sometimes you are thirsty; at other times, you just aren't. When you are thirsty, you crave something to drink. When you are hungry, you crave something to eat. During periods of intense hunger, you are likely to seek, procure, and ingest food. When you've eaten too much food, you usually don't feel hungry. You are prone to have very little appetite when you are in the act of vomiting.

If you go without sleep for several days in a row, you are prone to experience feelings of fatigue, weariness, or even exhaustion. The longer you go without sleep, the more tired you are likely to become. When you are asleep, you don't know it. In fact, it's only after you've woken up that you know that you were.

You're the kind of person who derives pleasure from scratching an itch. Pain hurts you. In fact, you typically attempt to avoid pain. When you are too cold, you have a strong tendency to seek heat. When you are too hot, you try to cool down. When you feel sick, you desire to feel better. When having sex, you're the type of person who would prefer to have an orgasm, rather than not have one. You experience a sense of satisfaction, even pleasure, after relieving your bladder or bowels. You prefer the smell of your own excreta to that of other people's.

Many of your bodily processes have an "automatic" quality to them. For example, when engaging in strenuous physical activity, your heartbeat, blood pressure, and respiration increase—whether you like it or not. When your skin is cut, you are prone to bleed. You're the type of person who is likely to experience a "gagging" sensation whenever a foreign object (such as a stick, screwdriver, or cooking utensil) is shoved down your throat.

Personality Characteristics

You have many sides to your personality. There are some parts of your personality that you like more than others. Deep down, you have some pretty deep feelings. These feelings are likely to be much deeper than those feelings that are closer to the surface. When your feelings are hurt, you're the kind of person who doesn't like it. Given the choice, you'd rather feel good than bad. Sometimes you are happy; sometimes you aren't. You like feeling happy, but you don't like feeling lonely, depressed, or anxious. In fact, the more miserable you are, the more you dislike it. You are more critical of yourself than other people are of you.

Interpersonal Functioning

You are similar to other people in some ways, but not in other ways. There are many people whom you just do not know. You enjoy having the respect of others. You like some people more than others. When you lose someone dear to you, you are likely to feel sad. In your relationships with others, you're trying to strike a balance between autonomy and closeness. Deep down, you crave love and approval. You want to be understood. You don't want to be rejected. You are the kind of person who prefers not being ridiculed, mocked, or tortured by others.

Goals and Expectations

You wish that you could be more like the person who you really want to be. You wish that you had more control over your life. You want to accomplish more. You would prefer to be successful than unsuccessful.

Diagnostic Impressions

(Check as many as desired, depending on the clinician's theoretical orientation.)

_____ You have intrapsychic conflict

_____ You have control issues

_____ You have boundary issues

_____ You have trust issues

_____ You have self-esteem issues

_____ You have inner-child issues

_____ You have codependency issues

_____ You have issues around intimacy and commitment

_____ You have ambivalent feelings toward your parents

_____ You have maladaptive learning patterns

_____ You have unfinished business

_____ You have repressed introjects

_____ You are searching for meaning in life

_____ You are your own worst enemy

_____ You come from a dysfunctional family

_____ You have a biochemical imbalance

Future Prognosis

If you continue to live, you will grow older. The longer you live, the more experiences you are likely to have. You will always be older than your younger siblings. At some point in your future, you will be completely unable to talk, walk, or even breathe. And this condition will last for a very, *very* long time.

References

American Psychiatric Association. (1987). *Diagnostic and statistical manual of mental disorders* (3rd ed., rev.). Washington, DC: Author.

Oral Sadism and the Vegetarian Personality

Glenn C. Ellenbogen, Ph.D.

A review of the clinical literature on vegetarianism to date reveals that little attention has been given to the psychodynamic mechanisms that govern the behavior of those individuals who choose to restrict their diet to foods other than dead animals. Fruitlooper's (1895) case study of Julia V., a 39-year-old pregnant hysteric unable to refrain from regurgitating Wienerschnitzels, had first thrown light upon the meatless phenomenon, but Fruitlooper's contemporaries rejected his psychosexual interpretation of Wienerschnitzels and interest in his discovery soon waned. It was not until von Krankman, one of Fruitlooper's more brilliant students, a tireless theoretician and jogger and, later, founder of the "neo-Fruitloopian school" of psychoanalysis, that interest in vegetarianism was renewed.

The connection between vegetarianism and sadism was first highlighted in von Krankman's (1939) seminal paper, "A Treatise on the Psychodynamics of the Meatless Choice." Von Krankman theorized that consumption of vegetables, to the exclusion of sinewy flesh, represented a "fixation" at an "oral-sadistic stage" of development.[1]

The fixation is by the rigid cathexis of energy to but one category of objects represented.[2] While the vegetarian not so very often to

---

[1] I would like to thank Mr. Angelo Augratini, A.A., adjunct assistant instructor of European languages, Hempstead Community College, for his translation of this passage from von Krankman's original text.

[2] *Translator's note:* I kind of had some trouble translating a pretty short sentence that came after this one so I just left it out.

other equally erogenous zones these organic substances placed observed have been, so can we say that the use of these vegetables truly, no, almost exclusively, to the oral zone placed are! Also, have we a sadistic impulse with the vegetarian character. The man who kills animals for meat gives the pursued animal a chance to escape. How more and more sadistically cruel is the non-meat eating man. The keen theoretician must himself this question deeply ask—What is the likelihood that the tranquil carrot from its vicious predator successfully outrun can?

During his American lecture series, delivered at the New School for Social Research in the Fall of 1941, von Krankman (1942) introduced a refinement and expansion of his work, outlining the process by which the vegetarian defends himself against conscious awareness of his sadistic impulses.

The orally fixated vegetarian deals with his early prototypic loss of the love object through compensatory defense mechanisms, which serve to conceal from himself, significant others, and his Saturday night dates, his deep-seated feelings of anger, hostility, hatred, rage, and, to some extent, dislike for his fellow man. Nor is his like for women too keen. Since the vegetarian character identifies man with animals (and rightfully so), he utilizes the defense mechanisms of reaction formation, denial, and sublimation in order to portray a façade whereby he is perceived as loving man, the animal, and hence animals, while displacing his true oral-sadistic impulses onto the non-man non-animal—vegetables. Thus it is that the orally sadistic vegetarian character comes to take delight in aggressively consuming vegetables while zealously and defensively maintaining his *dis-taste* for animals.

Although von Krankman was making inroads in the exploration of the psychodynamics of the vegetarian character, it was not until his now famous 1947 Invited Psychoanalysts Address before the faculty and candidates of the prestigious Advanced Institute for Psychoanalytic Psychotherapy that his thinking was crystallized with the conceptualization of "the Vegetarian Personality." Von Krankman's long and arduous theorizing was finally complete.

The Vegetarian Personality is characterized by ruthless acts of an oral-sadistic nature directed against vegetables. Through a series of complex and difficult (even for the analyst) to understand processes, a tripartition of the ego develops. This splitting of the ego leads to the gradual emergence of three compartmentalized senses of reality— "the good-food," "the bad-food," and "the not-food." Vegetables are perceived as "the good-food" because engaging in the consummatory act does not threaten to unleash the underlying currents of anxiety. Animals are perceived as "the bad-food" because even the thought of devouring them is threatening enough to arouse the vegetarian's fear of dealing with his repressed oral-aggressive and oral-sadistic urges toward his fellow man. Finally, there is the primitive taboo against phylogenetic self-destruction, so that man himself becomes "the not-food" and the impulse toward cannibalism is successfully defended against.

Von Krankman's tragic and untimely death from ingestion of poisonous mushrooms deprived the psychoanalytic community of a great mind. Nonetheless, his pioneering work in the area of oral sadism and the Vegetarian Personality had an enormous impact upon the field of psychoanalysis, prompting, if not a great deal of research, or any research for that matter, at least a great deal of heated debate among psychoanalysts.

It was a fitting tribute to von Krankman's greatness as a theoretician, clinician, and taxpayer that members of the American Psychiatric Association, in revising their outdated *Diagnostic and Statistical Manual of Mental Disorders (DSM),* spontaneously chose, upon unanimous recommendation of the Task Force on Nomenclature and Statistics, and at the adamant urging of the American Psychological Association, to incorporate von Krankman's work into their newly revised third edition, the *DSM-III.* The influence of von Krankman's penetrating thinking is clearly evident in the passage from the *DSM-III* reproduced below.

301.85 Vegetarian Personality Disorder

The essential feature is a Personality Disorder in which there is a severe preoccupation with food consumption, schizoid-like inability to empathize with certain living organisms (usually vegetables) within the environment, hypersensitivity to issues revolving around food ingestion, paranoid suspiciousness concerning the content of the dinner plate, and impaired social relationships, particularly in restaurant settings, due to rigidity in eating patterns.

Associated features. Individuals with this disorder usually are unable to express anger, hostility, or aggressiveness toward others, but fare well in expressing such feelings toward vegetables. Because of these people's intense preoccupations with food, they commonly have impaired social relationships and often they attempt to band together in self-help groups, called "food collectives." The rigidity of their eating behavior tends to contribute to their social impairment, and individuals with this disorder are frequently known to seek out partners who suffer from the same disorder.

Impairment. Eating behavior, by definition, is severely compartmentalized and rigid. Social relationships usually become impaired, as the individual gets into arguments with others over where to dine. While occupational functioning is rarely disturbed, the individual with this disorder usually brings lunch or buys a yogurt to go.

Complications. A common complication is Unintentional Substance Use Disorder, with toxicity appearing in the form of "MSG overdose" from eating in Chinese restaurants too often.

Predisposing factors. Finicky eating patterns in childhood may in some way be associated with the onset of this disorder in later adolescence or early adulthood, although the relationship is not clearly established.

Prevalence. This disorder appeared to be fairly common beginning in the late 1960s and continuing into the 1970s, but it seems to be tapering off.

Sex ratio. This disorder is diagnosed about equally among men and women.

Differential diagnosis. In **Paranoid Personality Disorder** there is, by definition, pervasive and systematic mistrust of people, whereas the **Vegetarian Personality Disorder** involves mistrust specifically related to the content of the dinner plate. In both the **Schizoid Personality Disorder** and **Narcissistic Personality Disorder,** conspicuous absence of any ability to empathize is a primary feature, whereas the **Vegetarian Personality Disorder** is characterized by an ability to empathize, at least on a superficial level, with other people and related animals.

Diagnostic Criteria for Vegetarian Personality Disorder

A. Loss of the love object early in life without subsequent resolution of at least five of the following emotions toward the love object:

    (1) anger
    (2) hostility
    (3) rage
    (4) hatred
    (5) dislike

B. Onset of the disorder in late adolescence or early adulthood.

C. Rigidity in eating patterns.

D. Inability to empathize with certain living organisms within the environment as indicated by:

    (1) an overconcern for the feelings and physical well-being of animals (e.g., verbalizing that it is "animalistic" to eat animals)

    (2) a conspicuous lack of empathy for the feelings of murdered vegetables (e.g., verbalizing, "But vegetables don't have feelings!")

E. Paranoid and hypervigiliant preoccupation with the oral zone and food consumption, as manifested by at least one of the following:

   (1) hypersensitivity to the issue of food ingestion

   (2) paranoid suspiciousness about food content:

      (a) individual thinks that there are pieces of dead animals on his plate

      (b) in advanced stages of the disorder, individual suspects that there are minuscule animal by-products mixed in with his food

F. Impairment of social and interpersonal relationships as indicated by at least one of the following:

   (1) decreased socializing at restaurants with friends because of the individual's arguing over where to dine

   (2) need to join a self-help group (e.g., a "food collective")

   (3) socializing exclusively with individuals also diagnosed as suffering from the Vegetarian Personality Disorder

G. "MSG overdose" from eating in Chinese restaurants too often.

References

American Psychiatric Association. (1980). *Diagnostic and statistical manual of mental disorders* (3rd ed.). Washington, DC: Author.

Fruitlooper, Seymour. (1895). *A case study of hysterical reactions to Schnitzels, breaded and unbreaded.* Vienna: University of Vienna Press.

Von Krankman, Ernst. (1939). A treatise on the psychodynamics of the meatless choice: Carrots, celery, lettuce, tomatoes, and sundry other organic vegetable substances—You call that dinner? *Journal of the Viennese Psychoanalytic Society, 21,* 312–384. (Also in *Haus und Garten,* 1939 [February], Berlin.)

Von Krankman, Ernst (1942). *Introductory lectures on the psychogenesis of taste and dis-taste in the orally-sadistic vegetarian character: Theoretical food for thought.* New York: Norton & Co.

Von Krankman, Ernst (1947). Splitting of the ego in the Vegetarian Personality: The "good-food," the "bad-food," and the "not-food." *Journal of Polymorphous Perversity, 38,* 412–437.

Understanding the Psychological Report: Differences Between What Clinicians Write and What They Really Mean

Loreto R. Prieto
University of Iowa

The discrepancy between what people truly mean and what they communicate to others, and the dire consequences that can result from such miscommunications, has received much attention in the pages of the *Journal of Polymorphous Perversity*. For example, Feingold (1990, 1992a) warned that graduate students who fail to recognize the underlying messages of their graduate advisors risk an abrupt and untimely end to their academic careers. In a similar vein, Pierce (1990) noted that doctoral candidates face failing their oral defense if they do not pay adequate attention to the subtext of the dissertation committee's verbalizations. Piersma (1990) cautioned that disaster will result if internship site interviewers take letters of recommendation at face value, instead of reading between the lines. Feingold (1992b) clarified how beginning professors risk being denied tenure by misinterpreting the statements of their graduate students. Most recently, Gawthrop (1993) noted that patients could suffer negative therapeutic outcomes if they do not recognize the disparity between their therapists' verbalizations and their therapists' underlying messages.

All too often, mental health professionals, when faced with reading psychological reports, fail to correctly interpret the latent messages conveyed therein. In the present paper, the author provides key interpretations to statements appearing in the psychological reports of clinicians. It is hoped that a clearer understanding of what clinicians really mean in their psychological reports will ensure that

16

mental health professionals will pick up on all of the subtle, and not-so-subtle, cues in these reports, thereby avoiding the possibility of mistakenly accepting into treatment "difficult" patients or those who lack excellent insurance coverage.

What the Clinician Writes	What the Clinician Means
This clinician examined the patient for one hour.	The examination took 40 minutes, but we bill by the hour.
The patient approached the interview in a cooperative manner.	The patient answered all of my questions, including the embarrassing ones.
The patient's affect was constricted in range, incongruent with the content of speech, and grounded within a dysphoric mood.	The patient did not laugh at my jokes.
The patient's rate of speech was normal.	The patient spoke in a manner that gave me time to take notes.
The patient's marital relationship appears appropriate, functional, and secure.	The patient and his wife fight about the same stuff my wife and I do.
The patient leads an irresponsible and carefree life.	Boy, am I jealous.
The patient engages in superficial sexual relationships with multiple partners without establishing meaningful emotional ties.	Amazing. I never did that well when I was single.

What the Clinician Writes	What the Clinician Means
The patient has an erratic work history.	The patient hasn't been stuck in as many crappy jobs as I've been.
The patient denies any substance use.	Yeah, right.
The patient has a significant history of extensive substance abuse.	Better keep the patient's number in the Rolodex for the next staff party.
The psychological test results are inconclusive.	The computer scoring service lost the patient's MMPI in the mail.
The patient took an inordinate amount of time to complete the assessment measure.	I had to stay late and missed my bus.
The patient was not goal oriented and needed frequent encouragement during testing.	The patient couldn't even handle a measly seven-hour testing session.
Testing was not indicated for this patient.	The patient has no insurance.
The patient was unresponsive to empathy.	The patient refused to accept my only slightly used handkerchief to dry his tears.
The patient displayed a remarkable acuity for environmental stimulus cues within interpersonal interaction.	The patient complimented me on my new suit.

What the Clinician Writes	What the Clinician Means
The patient demonstrated good conceptual, abstraction, and judgment skills.	The patient bought my self-help book and liked it.
The patient was histrionic and demanding.	The patient was shocked at my fees and asked if there was a sliding scale.
The patient shows an ability to meet social demands.	The patient didn't mind that I kept him waiting in the lobby for 20 minutes.
The patient was oppositional and unable to appropriately respond to social interaction.	The patient did not accept the appointment time that worked best for me.
This patient may benefit from referral to group therapy.	Talk about disturbed—there's no way I'm treating this guy!
This patient appears to be dealing with a complex clinical pathology that might possibly be ameliorated by a regimen of intensive, carefully executed psychotherapeutic intervention.	I can manage this one.

References

Feingold, A. (1990). Understanding your advisor: A survivor's guide for beginning graduate students. *Journal of Polymorphous Perversity, 7*(1), 12–14.

Feingold, A. (1992a). Understanding your advisor II: More survival tips for fledgling graduate students unfamiliar with interpreting "advisor-speak." *Journal of Polymorphous Perversity, 9*(1), 10–11.

Feingold, A. (1992b). Understanding your doctoral students: A guide for beginning professors. *Journal of Polymorphous Perversity, 9*(2), 9–10.

Gawthrop, J. (1993). Understanding your therapist: A primer for patients entering psychotherapy for the first time. *Journal of Polymorphous Perversity, 10*(1), 7–8.

Pierce, D. (1990). Understanding your doctoral dissertation committee: A survivor's guide for advanced graduate students. *Journal of Polymorphous Perversity, 7*(2), 19–20.

Piersma, H. L. (1990). Further advances in the professional psychology internship selection process: Interpretive guidelines for letters of reference. *Journal of Polymorphous Perversity, 7*(2), 10–11.

Critical *DSM-III-R* Axis II Differential Diagnostic Issues: How Many Personality Disorders Does It Take to Change a Lightbulb?

Jerry L. Jennings, Ph.D.

By now, every self-respecting psychotherapist knows how many therapists it takes to change a lightbulb,[1] right? But have you ever wondered how many Axis II personality disorders it takes to handle that classic problem? Let's take a look.

- How many Narcissistic Personality Disorders does it take to change a lightbulb?
  Just one—to hold the lightbulb, but he has to wait for the whole world to revolve around him.

- How many Borderline Personality Disorders does it take to change a lightbulb?
  Just one—to threaten suicide if you don't change it for her.

- How many Obsessive Compulsive Personality Disorders does it take to change a lightbulb?
  Just one—but he has to check it a hundred times, once for each watt.

- How many Passive Aggressive Personality Disorders does it take to change a lightbulb?
  "Oops! I can't believe I broke the *last* one. I guess you'll just have to sit in the dark, Honey."

---

[1] Just one—but only if the lightbulb really *wants* to change.

21

- How many Dependent Personality Disorders does it take to change a lightbulb?
None. She's still clinging to the old lightbulb.

- How many Histrionic Personality Disorders does it take to change a lightbulb?
"You want *me* to change lightbulbs?! I could burn my hand! I could be electrocuted! I could fall off of the ladder and be paralyzed for life! You don't *love* me anymore!"

- How many Self-Defeating Personality Disorders does it take to change a lightbulb?
Just testing you . . . We're waiting for the *DSM-IV* on that one!

- How many postal workers does it take to change a lightbulb?
Oh, I'm sorry, aren't *all* postal workers by definition personality disordered?

Free the *DSM-IV*

Judith Schlesinger, Ph.D.

The *DSM-IV (Diagnostic and Statistical Manual of Mental Disorders, Fourth Edition)* was coming in June—the new Bible of mental disorders and reimbursements. Because of the controversy surrounding its predecessor, the *DSM-III-R,* also published by the American Psychiatric Association (APA), I was assigned to interview one of the chief editors, Dr. Richard Shpritzer. My mission: to see if things were different this time around.

Our group is called PLOTZING (People Leery of the Zeitgeist in New Guidelines [in Mental Health]). Our concern: that the new manual would contain more politics than science.

"Oh, no," said Shpritzer when I brought the matter up, "this time, we asked everybody for their opinions. Jelly bean?"

"No, thanks," I said.

I looked around his office, which was large, airy, and dominated by stacks of books in proof—the *DSM-IV* itself, the *DSM-IV Sourcebook,* the *DSM-IV Notebook,* the *DSM-IV Guidebook,* the *DSM-IV Casebook,* the *DSM-IV Coloring Book (Kategories for Kids),* and the *DSM-IV Diagnosis-a-Day Desk Calendar.*

He saw me looking. "You like this stuff?" he asked, smiling. "The APA hasn't had to raise its dues in years." He showed me the coloring book. "This one's my favorite. Here, look at this picture of an Obsessive Compulsive Disorder. It really captures its essence, don't you think?"

He put down the book, which, I noticed, was half colored in, and took another handful of candy. "You're never too young to understand science. Even with all their problems, we're still behind the Russians, you know."

"But is science what we're talking about?" I wondered. "The *DSM-III-R* was built on political trade-offs—categories put in or thrown out, changed and bartered, depending on which pressure groups were squawking. I can think of at least six examples right now . . ."

"Squawking? That's absurd!" declared Shpritzer. "Squawking has no place in science. Look . . ." He picked up the order form for the *DSM-IV* and its accessories.

"See this, right here? It refers to our 'open process' and the 'quality and diversity' of our participants. There's no squawking when there's full inclusion. I think we even let the psychologists vote this time. It was a swell group. Jelly bean?"

"No, really, thanks. Diversity's important, sure, but it still sounds like the science-by-consensus thing all over again."

"Then read our *Sourcebook,* if you're so interested. That's where the empirical data and rationale are." He was getting agitated: grabbing more and more jelly beans. He ate only the red ones, and threw the rest away.

"And about that *Sourcebook,* Dr. Shpritzer," I said, "if you really want people to understand the scientific basis for the *DSM-IV,* why price the *Sourcebook* at more than twice the *DSM-IV* itself, with no option to get it in paperback? What are you hiding?"

"We are hiding nothing," he said, icily, "because we have nothing to hide. In fact, our market research shows that most clinicians have no interest in empirical matters at all. They have enough trouble getting the codes and Axes right."

"And besides," he continued, "this is the 90s. There's science, but there's also empowerment. We have to be sensitive, you know. After all," he leaned forward, "we *are* healers. We don't want to make things *worse* for people."

"I'm glad you mentioned that, Sir, because . . ." Suddenly his attention became focused on the window. One could hear chanting from the street. I couldn't quite make out the words.

"Oh, no, not again," he groaned, as he picked up the phone. "Excuse me a minute."

"No problem," I said. I touched up my notes and scanned the

bookcases. There was the usual batch of Freud and Jung, Rank and Adler, Krantz and Steele—along with an interesting collection of new titles: *The Therapist Giveth and Taketh Away: False Memory Syndrome; Diagnosis as a Political Act; Science Can Be Friendly;* and *Who Sez?*

The chant grew louder: the people were yelling, "Free the DSM Four! Free the DSM Four!" A lot of people.

Shpritzer shut the window and got back on the phone. "I thought you said we were going to include Frustrated Entitlement in the main section," he growled. "No, these guys won't go for it. . . . Yeah. . . . No, we can't. . . . Hey, that Late Luteal Phase Dysphoric Disorder almost sandbagged the whole thing, remember? . . . What? . . . Who? . . . Well, do what you can."

He hung up, frowning, and reached for his beans.

"Dr. Shpritzer . . ." I began, but he seemed distracted, chewing, staring into space, and playing with a new *DSM-IV* key chain ("Keys to the Mind"—$6.95, plus shipping and handling).

He looked at me, frowning again. "You still here? Listen, I really don't have time to continue this interview right now." I could tell he was rattled. He was spitting out the red jelly beans, and eating the rest.

And despite the closed window, the noise below was steadily increasing.

"Free the DSM Four!" was suddenly joined by a new chant: "Two, four, six, eight, you don't hafta medicate!" A siren sounded in the distance.

"Listen to them!" Dr. Shpritzer said. "It doesn't matter how many meetings you have, they still don't understand." He sighed. "Excuse me: I'm going to have to make some more calls."

"Just one more question, please. What was the role of political correctness in creating the *DSM-IV?*"

He looked at me, his eyes narrowing. "Say, what is this PLOTZ-ING thing anyway?" he asked. "How many are you, and what do you want? I'm a busy man."

I gave him our official speech: "We have about 10,000 members. Our issues include the arbitrary nature of diagnosis and treatment, and the fact that there are too many financial and political influences on what's supposed to be a science."

"Supposed to be? *Supposed* to be? Young lady, you can tell your PLOTZING friends that we adhered to the strictest standards of scientific rigor in compiling our diagnostic criteria!" He glared at me. "Have you ever heard of consensual validation?"

"Well sure, but . . ."

"And don't you think there are thousands of people out there who are suffering because of how others perceive them?"

"Yes, but . . ."

"So why shouldn't they have their own category and be able to be reimbursed for treatment?"

"Not being 'liked' is a mental disorder?"

"It is now," he said proudly. "It's called the Dangerfield Dysphoric Disorder; it's also known, informally, as the 'I Can't Get No Respect' Syndrome. No reason why we can't have a little humor in our humanity, right?" he chuckled.

"I heard there's also a category called the Milli Vanilli Syndrome, for people who let others speak for them?"

"That's in the section for future study, but, yes, we believe it may be a viable clinical entity."

I consulted my notes. "The Baby Boomer Sudden Mortality Recognition and Regret for the Paths Not Taken Dysphoric Disorder?"

He smiled. "It's a mouthful, yes, but we're working on it. Lots of reports coming in on that one. Jelly bean?"

"I'm trying to cut down, thanks. Organic Brain Syndrome Not Otherwise Specified But Possibly Due To Backward Baseball Caps?"

"I told you, we wanted to include everyone. And, yes, there is some very impressive evidence connecting cognitive problems with habitual cap reversal."

Meanwhile, the protest downstairs was intensifying—they'd added a bullhorn and a bass drum. "FREE THE DSM FOUR! FREE THE DSM FOUR!" blended with a new chant from a group on the periphery: "Managed care, mangled care, get Big Brother out of our hair!"

Dr. Shpritzer got up from his desk and went to the window. His eyes fastened on one of the group. "Oh no, I went to medical school with him. This is really getting out of hand."

Turning to me, he said, "Look, it's been nice chatting with you, but I really must get back to work now. And you must go back to PLOTZING."

"I intend to," I replied. "Thanks for your time." I shook his sticky hand, and before I'd even left the room, he was back on the phone again.

"Stop the presses!" he commanded. "They're back!"

Colonphilia: A Grammatical Personality Disorder Involving the Excessive Use of the Colon

Lawrence C. Katz, M.S.
Loyola University of Chicago

An extensive review of any body of literature in the field of psychology reveals the emergence of a disturbing malady prevalent among researchers: an uncontrollable urge to use a colon in the titles of their works. This appears to be a chronic disorder with a deteriorating course, if left untreated.

Introduction

The colon is primarily a mark of introduction, informing the reader that the preceding statement is about to be explained, amplified, or summarized. A colon may be appropriately used to separate titles and subtitles (Fowler & Aaron, 1989). However, this seemingly innocent usage may lead to a compulsion among those who write and publish, such that one becomes hopelessly incapable of completing a scholarly work without slapping some wordy colon-separated label on the title page.

For the researcher addicted to colons, life is an endless maze of extensions and elaborations. Hans Awf (1992), in his paper "A Case Study of Colonphilia with an Obstinate Researcher: Mostly Interventions that I Think are Pretty Good and Treatment Recommendations and a Discussion Section that is Not as Well-Written Because My Graduate Assistant Did It," describes a once prominent professor who became so obsessed with colons that he could only speak in elaborated sentences. An illustrative example follows:

Hans: Hello, Doctor.
Dr. X: Hi, how are you?: A salutation and rhetorical question.
Hans: How is your research going?
Dr. X: It's going fine: An obvious lie. I still can't seem to keep the titles down to an acceptable length: Confession of a colonphiliac. It's quite distressing: A desperate cry for help. I hope I can get over this: Thinly veiled self-doubt.
Hans: I think I can help.
Dr. X: That would be great: Reaction to an empty promise that this fool is unlikely to be able to fulfill.

This segment clearly demonstrates how an excessive reliance on the colon may become debilitating to interpersonal relationships.

Etiology

Some psychoanalytic theorists (e.g., Anna, Lizum, & Billum, 1992; Onda, Couch, & Spillit, 1991) posit that colonphilia stems from a fixation at the oedipal phase of development. According to this theory, the colonphiliac feels the need to insert his upright phallus between the primary, all-powerful part of the title (the father) and the supportive, nurturing part of the title (the mother).

Cognitive theorists (Hunt & Beck, 1991) point to the irrational belief system behind the use of the colon. They propose that researchers tend to believe, "If I don't extend this title, my work will be dismissed, because people will have to read the article to find out what it's really about, and no one will want to do that because it's quite meaningless and because I'm worthless. If people dismissed this work, it would be awful, because I would forever be worthless. Therefore, I must include a colon to extend this title."

Treatment

Given the opposing etiological assumptions across the various theoretical orientations, no consensus exists as to the optimal course of therapy for colonphilia. Psychodynamic theorists recommend a course of approximately 40 years to life, consisting of three one-hour sessions per week. The goal is resolution of the oedipal conflict through illumination of the displacement of unresolved castration fears, with neurotic ego defenses and fetishist libidinal impulses sublimated primarily through the transferential phallic fixation.

Cognitive therapists attempt to challenge the underlying irrational belief that having no one read their works would be "awful." Attempts to convince researchers that their articles are worthwhile and interesting enough to be widely read even without a cumbersome title tend to be ineffective, because this perspective has no basis in reality. Therefore, cognitive treatment aims to encourage colonphiliacs to just accept that their works are unlikely to be read, with or without an expanded title. The patient is given instructions that, when titling an article, he or she is to say, "Stop. Nobody will read this anyway, and that's okay. I might as well make this title brief. I do not *have* to use a colon."

Behavioral theorists favor an even more direct approach. Studies have shown that administering an electric shock to subjects as they reach for the colon key on a keyboard significantly reduces the length and general wordiness of titles. For a complete review, see Zappum and Good, 1990.

Finally, international Colonphiliacs Anonymous (CA) groups, focusing on the addictive nature of the disorder, are beginning to form. These groups have developed a 12-step treatment program, including such therapeutic landmarks as, "Acceptance: I am powerless over the colon" and "Relinquishment of responsibility: There is a higher grammatical power." Unlike other 12-step support groups, this program actually takes tokens away from participants for saying, "My name is John: I am a colonphiliac."

Proposed DSM-IV Criteria for Colonphilia

Diagnostic Criteria for Colonphilia

A. The individual is chronically and progressively unable to resist impulses to expand titles with the use of the colon.

B. The use of the colon compromises, disrupts, or damages family, personal, and vocational pursuits, as indicated by at least three of the following:

(1) Titles of works are so long that they exceed the limits for Abstracts in most journals.

(2) Loss of work due to absenteeism and inability to meet submission deadlines. This may be a result of excessive deliberation over a final title, given the multitude of seemingly good possibilities afforded by the use of a colon.

(3) Disruption in relationships due to the overly revealing use of colons in speech (e.g., "I love you: An expected prerequisite to sexual relations").

(4) Inability to title written works (including journal articles, grocery lists, birthday cards, etc.) without the use of a colon.

C. The colon use is not due to another Grammatical Personality Disorder.

The recognition of colonphilia as a debilitating and annoying disorder resulting in excessively wordy titles and the conceptualization of an optimally effective treatment are critical: The time has come.

References

Anna, U., Lizum, A., & Billum, I. (1992). Sticking the phallic colon between mother and father: A grammatical personality disorder resulting from the Oedipal conflict but treatable with intensive and prolonged psychoanalysis. *Journal of Psychoanalytic Psychobabble, 69*(6), 969.

Awf, H. (1992). A case study of colonphilia with an obstinate researcher: Mostly interventions that I think are pretty good and treatment recommendations and a discussion section that is not as well-written because my graduate assistant did it. *Journal of Quick and Easy Case Studies, 1*(1), 1.

Fowler, H. R., & Aaron, J. E. (1989). *The Little, Brown Handbook: Fourth Ed.* Glenview, IL: Scott, Foresman.

Hunt, U., & Beck, I. M. (1991). The etiology of colonphilia: The irrational belief that, if I don't extend this title, my work will be dismissed, because people will have to read the article to find out what it's really about, and no one will want to do that because it's quite meaningless and because I'm worthless and if people dismissed this work, it would be awful, because I would forever be worthless and, therefore, I must include a colon to extend this title. *Mental Masturbation, 1*(23), 45.

Onda, U., Couch, D., & Spillit, Y. (1991). Dysfunctional colon insertion in titles of psychological works: Why not just kill Dad, sleep with Mom, blind yourself, and get it over with already? *Psychologist's Briefs, 69*(2), 69.

Zappum, I., & Good, Y. B. (1990). A review of behavioral techniques for the treatment of colonphilia: Some shocking findings to keep researchers on their toes. *Journal of Sanctioned Torture, 66*(6), 666.

Toward the Application of Diagnostic Criteria to Personality-Disordered Psychotherapy Patients: Understanding Axis II of the *DSM-III-R* as It Has Never Been Understood Before

David J. Robinson, M.D.
St. Joseph's Health Center
London, Ontario, Canada

With the advent of the American Psychiatric Association's (1987) most recent tome on psychiatric diagnosis—the *Diagnostic and Statistical Manual of Mental Disorders, 3rd Edition, Revised (DSM-III-R)*—mental health professionals have been treated to a new classification system, one in which various mental disorders are coded on different "Axes," with "Personality Disorders" confined to Axis II. Whereas the *DSM-III-R*'s Axis II focuses on the application of diagnostic criteria to the behaviors of individuals in general, the author presents here the seminal work on the application of diagnostic criteria to the behaviors of psychotherapy patients in specific, to the way in which these individuals relate to the therapist and to the therapy process. It is hoped that these specific criteria for diagnosing personality-disordered psychotherapy patients will help clinicians everywhere pigeonhole, treat, and bill their patients more quickly.

Paranoid Personality Disorder

Before session	Checks to see if followed, confirms authenticity of therapist's diploma

33

Waiting room reading	Looks for *Soldier of Fortune* magazine
Appearance	Horn rimmed glasses with rear-view mirrors
Employment	Full-time projectionist
Fantasizes about . . .	Demanding a full explanation of therapist's jokes
Relationship with animals	Questions pet dog's fidelity
Talks about during session	Questions partner's fidelity
Relationship with therapist	Questions therapist's fidelity
Behavior during session	Complains about lack of warmth in office
Leaves with therapist	Scrapbook of injustice collection

Schizoid Personality Disorder

Before session	Walks to session, takes back alleys
Waiting room reading	Avoids waiting room, reads *Abstract Science* magazine in hallway
Appearance	Stove-pipe pants and wide tie
Employment	Runs a bowling alley between 1–7 a.m.
Fantasizes about . . .	Pines away for philosophy course instructor
Relationship with animals	Brings dog to session
Talks about during session	Marvels over new surveillance cameras in building entrance
Relationship with therapist	Asks therapist to play *Dungeons and Dragons*
Behavior during session	Teeters on edge (of chair)
Leaves with therapist	Copy of latest fad diet, shows collection of mail order catalogues

Schizotypal Personality Disorder

Before session	Reads palms, tea leaves, and Tarot cards of others in waiting room
Waiting room reading	*Astrology Weekly*
Appearance	Tin foil hat, shirt stapled together, unpaired socks
Employment	Developer for a UFO landing pad
Fantasizes about . . .	A weekly show with the Canadian Thought Broadcasting Corporation
Relationship with animals	Laments that pet budgie is dead, despite séances
Talks about during session	Starts session by talking to self
Relationship with therapist	Casts a spell on the therapist
Behavior during session	Rubs camphor on knee to prevent spleen cancer
Leaves with therapist	Book on neologistics—"How to Call 'Em As I See 'Em"

Histrionic Personality Disorder

Before session	Flirts with others in waiting room
Waiting room reading	Does quiz from fashion magazines
Appearance	Matching earrings, purse, nails, and shoes
Employment	Cosmetician
Fantasizes about . . .	Being a sex therapist
Relationship with animals	Owns 3 fluffy white cats: Puffy, Buffy, and Muffy
Talks about during session	Gives quiz results to therapist
Relationship with therapist	Writes best-selling novels based on sex fantasies with therapist

Behavior during session	Faints when quiz results are interpreted
Leaves with therapist	Perfumed handkerchief, with private phone number in lipstick, on chair

Narcissistic Personality Disorder

Before session	Grooming in a portable mirror
Waiting room reading	*GQ;* lies to others that a model with a close resemblance is really him
Appearance	Silk suit, cubic zirconium cufflinks, alligator belt
Employment	Men's store as a window dresser
Fantasizes about . . .	What he's like in bed
Relationship with animals	Walks friend's Afghan in order to meet women
Talks about during session	Every sentence begins with "I . . ."
Relationship with therapist	Self-appointed fashion consultant to therapist
Behavior during session	Behaves as if session were being filmed
Leaves with therapist	A flyer for a 50%-off sale from his clothing store

Antisocial Personality Disorder

Before session	Holds up the pharmacy in the lobby of the therapist's building
Waiting room reading	Steals magazines, leaves old copies of *Playboy* with centerfolds missing
Appearance	Sideburns, muscle shirt, cowboy boots, tattoo

Employment	Worked on "career" since childhood
Fantasizes about . . .	Sexual encounter with probation officer
Relationship with animals	Shows the innate sensitivity of a taxidermist
Talks about during session	Starts each sentence with "!@#$%&* . . ."
Relationship with therapist	Pickpocketed therapist's calling card; placed several long distance calls
Behavior during session	Carves up armrest with switchblade, copies down **Histrionic**'s phone number
Leaves with therapist	Advice to get a car alarm

Borderline Personality Disorder

Before session	Has fight with ex-lover outside office
Waiting room reading	Castrates all pictures of men in magazines
Appearance	Dresses completely in black or white; today it's black
Employment	Summer camp counsellor
Fantasizes about . . .	Wants to sleep with therapist and therapist's partner
Relationship with animals	Sleeps with pet cat and stuffed teddy bear
Talks about during session	Smells perfume from **Histrionic,** goes into a rage
Relationship with therapist	Threatens blackmail after above sexual encounter
Behavior during session	Widens hole in chair made by **Antisocial**
Leaves with therapist	Weekly suicide note on way out of session

Avoidant Personality Disorder

Before session	Followed **Schizoid**'s route to the session; hoped they might meet
Waiting room reading	Rather than take a magazine someone else might want to look at, reads nothing
Appearance	Coordinates clothes with wallpaper in therapist's office
Employment	Model for "before" pictures in weightlifting ads
Fantasizes about . . .	Having Dale Carnegie reincarnated as his uncle
Relationship with animals	Trained dog to walk itself
Talks about during session	The best detours, exits, and off-ramps in the city
Relationship with therapist	Follows therapist daily, hides in shadows to protect car from **Antisocial**
Behavior during session	Spends most of session with head in lampshade
Leaves with therapist	*Invisible Man* comic book

Dependent Personality Disorder

Before session	Arrives from another therapist's office
Waiting room reading	Brings autographed self-help book written by yet another therapist
Appearance	Athletic shirt with "Just Take Me" on it—underneath a big fuzzy sweater
Employment	Food bank, pet hotel, block parent, neighborhood sandwich maker
Fantasizes about . . .	Chaining up therapist in home

Relationship with animals	Chains dog up inside house to prevent it from running away
Talks about during session	Nightmares after watching *Home Alone*
Relationship with therapist	Sits in therapist's car when **Avoidant** not watching it
Behavior during session	Moves chair next to therapist; tape records session for relaxation therapy.
Leaves with therapist	Invitation to dinner, every night for a month

Obsessive-Compulsive Personality Disorder

Before session	Washes hands before and after trip to washroom
Waiting room reading	Rearranges magazines, no time to read
Appearance	Ironed socks, pressed jeans, starched underwear
Employment	Molecule counter for a chemical company
Fantasizes about . . .	Not flushing the toilet
Relationship with animals	Has sent dog to obedience school for 8 years
Talks about during session	Reads therapist the new rules of conduct from work
Relationship with therapist	Demands therapist synchronize watch at start of each session
Behavior during session	Repairs hole in chair with pocket sewing kit
Leaves with therapist	Copy of an etiquette book

Passive-Aggressive Personality Disorder

| Before session | Arrives late, blames **Obsessive** for setting therapist's watch ahead |

Waiting room reading	Tears out articles of interest from magazines
Appearance	Models fashion after **Borderline;** except wears black and white together
Employment	Somewhere in government
Fantasizes about . . .	Being not disgruntled
Relationship with animals	Makes dog drag food home by itself
Talks about during session	Waits 5 seconds, interrupts therapist repeatedly, then forgets what to say
Relationship with therapist	Left wrong insurance number after forgetting it three times
Behavior during session	Somewhere between Miss Manners and the Terminator
Leaves with therapist	Gives notice of termination to secretary, after session

References

American Psychiatric Association. (1987). *Diagnostic and statistical manual of mental disorders* (3rd ed., rev.). Washington, DC: Author.

2
Psychotherapy

Understanding Your Therapist: A Primer for Patients Entering Psychotherapy for the First Time

John Gawthrop, M.A.

People often say one thing when they really mean something completely different. There may be dire consequences when a listener fails to correctly interpret the subtle nuances and meanings of a given message. For instance, Feingold (1990, 1992a) notes that the graduate student who fails to heed the latent messages of his or her graduate advisor may find a promising career ended in an abrupt and untimely manner. Similarly, Pierce (1990) cautions that the doctoral candidate risks failing the oral defense if the underlying messages of the dissertation committee go unacknowledged. Piersma (1990) predicts disastrous results if internship site interviewers take the content of letters of recommendation at face value, rather than accurately interpreting the subtext. Most recently, Feingold (1992b) outlines how beginning professors can ultimately be denied tenure if they misinterpret the meanings of their graduate students' statements.

Misinterpretations and resultant negative repercussions are not limited to the academic domain. In fact, in the therapy room—one of the most common clinical settings—it is vital that the patient accurately interpret the verbalizations of the psychotherapist if the patient is to facilitate positive therapeutic outcome: to make the therapist feel accomplished, effective, and successful. As a public service to psychotherapy patients everywhere, then, the author presents here insightful interpretations of "therapist-speak."

What Your Therapist Says	What Your Therapist Means
Who's telling you to swear like that?	I believe you want the exorcist down the hall.
May I ask who recommended me to you?	That's the last time I use that referral source!
Yes, I have a Ph.D.	Clearly, I'm the expert here and don't you forget it.
I have a sliding fee scale.	I take anything from cash to securities.
Your problem often takes years of therapy to overcome.	I'm investing in a condo in Maui.
I sense you're feeling hostile right now.	Put that gun down.
Let me tell you something from my own experience. . . .	Enough about you—let's talk about me.
Let's go over this again.	I wasn't listening.
This new medication will help you.	It's only been tested on baboons, but you *can't* get any worse, can you?
I'm not sure I follow you.	I've never heard anything so stupid in all my life.
I'd like to recommend a book to you.	I'd like to recommend my book to you.

What Your Therapist Says	What Your Therapist Means
If you take two of these, you'll feel much better.	If you take two of these, I'll feel much better.
You're absolutely right!	Of course you are, you're quoting me.
I don't mind going a bit over time if you don't.	I can't stand my next patient anyway.
What I'm hearing here is just an example of negative transference.	I don't have to sit here and take this crap.
Don't be concerned—I'm just showing you negative countertransference.	There—how do *you* like it?!
You deserve most of the credit for your progress.	I deserve most of the credit for your progress.
Maybe it would be better for you to ask *yourself* that question.	I haven't the foggiest idea.

References

Feingold, A. (1990). Understanding your advisor: A survivor's guide for beginning graduate students. *Journal of Polymorphous Perversity, 7*(1), 12–14.

Feingold, A. (1992a). Understanding your advisor II: More survival tips for fledgling graduate students unfamiliar with interpreting "advisor-speak." *Journal of Polymorphous Perversity, 9*(1), 10–11.

Feingold, A. (1992b). Understanding your doctoral students: A guide for beginning professors. *Journal of Polymorphous Perversity, 9*(2), 9–10.

Pierce, D. (1990). Understanding your doctoral dissertation committee: A survivor's guide for advanced graduate students. *Journal of Polymorphous Perversity, 7*(2), 19–20.

Piersma, H. L. (1990). Further advances in the professional psychology internship selection process: Interpretive guidelines for letters of reference. *Journal of Polymorphous Perversity, 7*(2), 10–11.

Streamlined Treatment in the Era of Managed Care: The Fast-Food-for-Thought Therapy Approach

Jane P. Sheldon, Ph.D.

In our hectic, fast-paced world, clients cannot always afford the time it takes for traditional therapy. Additionally, managed care companies have shown a growing reluctance to pay for therapy services that require more than a few sessions of treatment. This has led to the development of a new, time- and cost-effective therapeutic approach, which takes its cue from the fast food industry. The following case study illustrates the effectiveness of this new approach.

Therapist: Hello, may I help you, sir?

Client: Umm, yes, I'm here because things aren't going well with my job and I just don't know what to do.

Therapist: What would you like?

Client: To feel good and be happy in my life, that's what I'd like. That's why I'm here.

Therapist: Would you like a drink?

Client: Oh, no! Just because my mother was an alcoholic doesn't mean I'll be! There's no way I'll ever become like her!

Therapist: Is there something else I can do for you?

Client: Well, really the reason I'm here is because of my job. I'm just not satisfied at work and I'm constantly anxious.

Therapist?   Chicken?

Client: A little, I guess. I'm afraid to try things. I guess it's because I think I'll fail. And then work just piles up and I'm never on top of it. I guess you'd call me a procrastinator. I put things off, then they accumulate and suddenly I'm overwhelmed.

Therapist: Ketchup?

Client: Exactly. I'm always behind and never seem to be able to catch up. Now and then I'll finally get a job done, but for some reason I still can't relax. I can never let up for a moment.

Therapist: Super fries, sir?

Client: Oh, yeah! My supervisor fries my nerves. She's always breathing down my neck making sure I'm not slacking off. It's like having my mother around! Hey! I get it! She's just like my mom! No wonder I always feel so tense and incompetent at work! Wow, Doctor, you're great! I've only been here a few minutes, but I feel so satisfied!

Therapist: Anything else?

Client: No, that's all. Thanks a lot, Doctor.

Therapist: Thank you. Come again. Have a nice day.

The Implications of City, Town, Village, and Hamlet Names for Psychotherapeutic Treatment and Outcome: When Normal [IL] is Indicated and Looneyville [WV] Contraindicated

Ernst von Krankman, Ph.D.

One of the basic tenets of modern-day psychodynamic theory is that people—and psychotherapy patients—can have very different emotional reactions to the same or similar events. Capitalizing on the subjective manner in which people interpret reality, von Krankman (1989a, 1989b) generated several studies demonstrating that the surnames of psychologists and psychiatrists might be indicated or contraindicated in working with psychotherapy patients suffering from specific diagnostic presenting problems. For instance, he cited the depressed patient who had a negative emotional reaction (or − reaction) to the news of being assigned to a therapist named Dr. Downs. On the other hand, manic-depressive patients often experienced favorable first reactions (+ reactions) when assigned to a therapist named Dr. Balance. And then there were those really tough, questionable (?) diagnostic judgment calls where it was unclear whether the therapist's name was indicated or contraindicated. For example, how wise, von Krankman asked, would it be to assign a manic patient to Dr. Allbright?

However, subjective responses of patients with specific presenting problems are not limited just to the surnames of therapists; patients also may reveal a wide range of emotional reactions to the names of *locations*. For example, would a patient who has had a life-long history of bizarre behavior feel more positively disposed (or +) to being treated in (or perhaps even just moving to) the city of Normal (Illinois) than Looneyville (West Virginia)? (The question of whether a person born and raised in Normal [IL] does indeed evidence more mentally healthy attributes than one nurtured in

Looneyville [WV] is a highly complex one that is beyond the scope of the present paper.) But for a patient with a history of serious and prolonged depression, relocation to and/or treatment in Funk (Nebraska) would clearly be contraindicated (or −). And, it should be kept in mind once again that there are some really tough diagnostic judgment calls. For instance, card-playing gambling addicts may leap at the opportunity to undergo treatment in the town of New Deal (Tennessee), but the wisdom of choosing such a location is certainly questionable (or ?).

What other municipal names may be indicated or contraindicated for patients with various diagnostic presenting problems? In order to answer this question, and expanding upon the original pioneering work of von Krankman, the present author (von Krankman) performed an exhaustive (and exhausting) search of the literature—the 2345 pages of the official U.S. Post Office zip code directory (U.S. Postal Service, 1990). The resultant data are presented below.

Municipal Name (and State)	Indication	Diagnostic Presenting Problem
Allgood (AL)	+	Any patient
Ampere (NJ)	?	Patients given ECT
Barker (NY)	?	Tourette's disordered patients
Beltline (AL)	?	Eating disordered patients
Broadview (GA)	?	Male chauvinistic patients
Bryte (CA)	?	Learning disabled members of Mensa
Burnwell (AL)	?	Firesetters

Municipal Name (and State)	Indication	Diagnostic Presenting Problem
Canon (GA)	–	Impotent patients
Climax (CO)	?	Impotent patients
Cloudland (GA)	–	Depressives
Coburn (PA)	?	Two firesetters acting in unison
Confluence (KY)	?	Multiple personality disordered patients
Crossville (AL)	?	Paranoid schizophrenics with active religious delusions
Cut and Shoot (TN)	?	Psychotic patients experiencing command hallucinations instructing them to "Kill!"
Cut Off (LA)	?	Patients with castration anxiety
Deposit (NY) *also* Port Deposit (MD)	?	Encopretics
Downers Grove (IL) *also* Downsville (LA)	–	Depressives
Dozier (AL)	?	Narcoleptics

Municipal Name (and State)	Indication	Diagnostic Presenting Problem
Eek (AK)	?	Patients experiencing difficulty expressing intense emotion
El Mirage (AZ)	?	Schizophrenics with visual hallucinations
Enigma (GA)	?	Patients suffering from existential crises
False Pass (AK)	?	Patients with hysterical pregnancy
Flying H (NM)	?	Heroin addicts
Footville (WI)	?	Fetishists (foot)
Franktown (CO)	+	Patients who have learned to be communicative and straightforward with their feelings and thoughts
	−	Vegetarians opposed to consuming hot dogs
Free Soil (MI)	?	Encopretics
Froid (MT)	?	Learning disabled psychology majors unable to correctly spell "Freud"
Fruitland Park (FL)	?	Patients with homosexual panic

Municipal Name (and State)	Indication	Diagnostic Presenting Problem
Funk (NE)	–	Depressives
Goodview (VA)	?	Voyeurs
Goodyears Bar (CA)	?	Alcoholics
Grand Ledge (MI)	?	Suicidal patients
Grubville (MO)	?	Eating disordered patients
Gusher (UT)	?	Premature ejaculators
Hancock (IA)	?	Compulsive masturbators
Hilo (HI)	?	Manic-depressives
Hippo (KY)	?	Bulimics
Hungry Horse (MT)	?	Eating disordered patients
Hytop (AL)	?	Adolescent sneaker aficionados
Kayjay (KY)	?	Learning disabled who cannot correctly sequence letters of the alphabet
Kill Devil Hills (NC)	?	Floridly psychotic patients experiencing sinister delusions and hallucinations

Municipal Name (and State)	Indication	Diagnostic Presenting Problem
Leakesville (MS) *and* Leakey (TN)	?	Enuretics
Little Creek (DE) *also* Little River (AL)	?	Young enuretics
Lilburn (GA)	?	Toddler firesetters
Littleport (IA) *also* Lockport (LA)	?	Patients suffering from vaginismus
Load (KY)	?	Encopretics
Loco Hills (NM)	?	Patients with florid psychotic symptomatology
Lone Jack (MO) *also* Lone Pine (CA)	?	Schizoid personality disordered patients
Looneyville (WV)	?	*See* Loco Hills
Lovelady (TN) *also* Loveland (CO)	?	Nymphomanics
Lowpoint (IL)	–	Depressives
Lulu (FL)	?	*See* Loco Hills
McLean (IL) *also* McLeansboro (IL)	?	Anorectics of Scottish descent
Manley Hot Springs (AK)	?	Male patients experiencing homosexual panic

Municipal Name (and State)	Indication	Diagnostic Presenting Problem
Maybee (MI)	?	Patients suffering from existential dilemmas and unable to make decisions
Napolean (IN)	?	Schizophrenics
Needville (TN)	?	Dependent personality disordered patients
Newfoundland (KY)	?	Dissociative disordered patients
New Deal (TN)	?	Card-playing gambling addicted patients
New Hope (AR)	+	Depressives
New Market (AL)	?	Compulsive shoppers
New River (FL)	?	Children and adolescents exhibiting enuretic symptoms as a regressive behavior
New Sharon (IA)	?	Transsexual patients
Nodaway (IA)	?	Narcoleptics
Normal (IL) *also* Normalville (PA)	+	All patients
Nut Tree (CA) *also* Nuttsville (VA)	?	*See* Loco Hills

Municipal Name (and State)	Indication	Diagnostic Presenting Problem
Orderville (UT)	?	Obsessive compulsive disordered patients
Outing (MN)	?	Agoraphobics
Palm City (CA)	?	Kleptomaniacs
Paw Paw (IL)	?	Stutterers
Panorama City (CA)	?	Voyeurs
Parker (ID) *also* Parkmoor (CA)	?	Catatonics
Peculiar (MO)	?	Schizotypal personality disordered patients
Purgatory (CO)	?	Patients suffering from over-punitive superegos
Queen Creek (AZ) *also* Queen Valley (AZ)	?	Homosexuals manifesting feminine behavior
Rainbow City (AL)	?	Patients with a history of hallucinogen abuse
Red Bluff (CA)	?	Anorectic patients who no longer have menstrual flow
Rockwell (AR) *also* Rockwell City (IA)	?	Autistics

Municipal Name (and State)	Indication	Diagnostic Presenting Problem
Rough and Ready (CA)	?	Sadists and masochists
Sale City (GA)	?	Compulsive shoppers
Snug Harbor (MA)	?	Patients suffering from vaginismus
Soft Shell (KY)	?	Patients with poor ego defenses, particularly schizophrenics
South of the Border (SC)	?	*See* Loco Hills
Sugar City (CO)	?	Suicidal diabetics
Talking Rock (GA)	?	Schizophrenics experiencing auditory and visual hallucinations
Terminal Island (GA)	?	Patients with suicidal ideation
Thunderbolt (GA)	?	Patients given ECT
Tuba City (AZ)	?	Bulimics
Turtletown (TN)	?	Patients suffering from psychomotor retardation
Twig (MN)	?	Anorectics

Municipal Name (and State)	Indication	Diagnostic Presenting Problem
Typo (KY)	?	Patients prone to passive-aggressive accidents
Volcano (CA)	?	Explosive personality disordered patients
Wacker Drive (IL)	?	Compulsive masturbators
Walla Walla (WA)	?	Verbally perseverative patients
	?	Regressed patients imitating Fozzy Bear from Sesame Street
Wetmore (CO)	?	Unsuccessfully treated enuretics
Whale Pass (AK)	?	Patients attracted to, and actively engaged in flirting with, obese members of the opposite sex
Why (AZ)	?	Patients suffering from existential dilemmas
Wilburn (AZ)	?	Unbridled firesetters
Wynot (NE)	?	Oppositional adolescent patients

Future Directions

The author has highlighted here municipal names that may elicit strong emotional reactions from patients suffering from a wide range of presenting symptomatology. In previous papers, the author has explored the impact of therapist surname on the subjective reactions of therapy patients. It still remains to be seen what *interaction effects* may exist between location name and therapist surname. For instance, is it really a good idea for a newly trained therapist, Dr. Looney, to set up shop in Nut Tree (CA) if he plans on working with patients suffering from gross reality testing problems? Or for Dr. Overton to start seeing eating disordered patients in Beltline (AL)? And what of establishing a group practice in Gusher (UT), where premature ejaculators will be seen and treated by Drs. Popoff, Cummings, Getoff, and Quick?

No doubt studies to follow will investigate the impact that *street address* may have upon the emotional reactions of patients suffering from a variety of presenting problems. Then, too, there is the complex issue of street address as it *interacts* with municipal name and therapist surname. For example, certainly, Dr. Warm, a humanistic therapist concerned with presenting a positive mental health image, would be just as well advised to seek a therapy office on Helping Hand Avenue in Normal (IL) as Dr. Graves, specializing in treating suicidal patients, would be to avoid a practice on Dead End Lane in Farewell (AK). The street numbers themselves may form a significant component of the Street Address × Municipal Name × Therapist Surname interaction. The floridly paranoid schizophrenic patient preoccupied with sinister ruminations may react quite adversely to treatment rendered by Dr. Spyer of *666* Devil's Landing, Hell Gate (NY).

It should be obvious to the reader that there are not only many avenues still to be explored in this exciting field of nominal data, but many boulevards, streets, lanes, and alleys as well. Future researchers will find that the raw data for their investigations have already been systematically collected—in the form of 10,000-plus telephone books—and simply await refined analysis.

References

U.S. Postal Service. (1990). *National five-digit zip code & post office directory, 1990.* Washington, DC: Author.

von Krankman, E. (1989a). Therapist surname and the presenting problems of psychotherapy patients: Implications for treatment and therapy outcome. *Journal of Polymorphous Perversity, 6*(1), 16–23.

von Krankman, E. (1989b). Psychiatrist surname and the presenting problems of psychotherapy patients: Implications for treatment and therapy outcome. *Journal of Polymorphous Perversity, 6*(2), 3–9.

Antidotes to Your Shrink's Falling Asleep During the Therapy Session: A Patient's Guide to Keeping the Therapist's Attention

William Goodenough, Ph.D.

Let's face it. Patients on the analytic couch expect their analysts to be tuned into their every utterance, but sometimes analysts, comfortably seated in their black leather chairs, positioned behind the couch and out of the patient's field of vision, do doze off, leaving patients free associating to no one. Given that the chance of the analyst's making a timely interpretation, or any interpretation at all for that matter, is nil if the analyst has been snoozing and was oblivious to the patient's verbalizations, the analytic patient is at great risk of not getting "good value" for the money during the therapy hour. It is vital, then, that the analytic patient learn effective ways of keeping the analyst in a heightened state of alertness in order to prevent such nodding off. This paper presents concrete tactics that will ensure retaining the analyst's attention.

Insist that one of your *other* personalities already paid last month's therapy bill.

Tell your therapist that you had a critical dream last night, but someone stole it from your head on the way to the session.

Begin to drool.

Ask your therapist if malpractice insurance covers patients who jump out of the therapy room window.

Lie down *under* the couch.

Ask if your therapist gives triple-A discounts.

Greet your therapist naked.

Express concerns that you are not narcissistic enough.

Wonder aloud what colors smell like.

Come to the session precisely on time, then apologize for being so late.

Suddenly begin free associating in a foreign language, preferably an unrecognizable one.

Bark.

Note aloud that your previous five therapists had more comfortable couches.

Shout "Eureka!" after your therapist makes an interpretation.

As your therapist hands you the therapy bill, put on a pair of latex rubber gloves to accept it.

Sit up on the couch suddenly and ask your therapist, "Hey, why are you so manic today?"

Comment that you are Jewish, and you are deeply committed to tithing 10 percent of your income to the church.

Hold a mirror up to your therapist's face just as he is making an interpretation.

As you enter the session, call your therapist Sigmund while slapping him on the back. (If your therapist is a woman, all the better!)

Play dead.

Note that you are a workaholic and that the only reason you have not killed yourself so far is that you couldn't fit it into your schedule. As you are leaving the session, casually comment that you forget to mention that this morning you were laid off by your employer.

Roll off the couch.

(For *male* patients only): Ask your therapist, "Is it cold in here, or is it just that time of the month?"

Ask if your therapist accepts the Discover card.

A Therapist's Guide to Proper Conduct During the Therapy Hour: The Fine Art of Appearing to Care

Susan C. Jenkins, M.D.
Associates in Psychiatry and Psychology

Many aspects of psychotherapy are eloquently addressed throughout the arduous training process of becoming a psychologist, psychiatrist, or clinical social worker. Learning to spell and pronounce words such as "psychopharmacotherapeutics" is certainly important, as is the careful attention given to observation of the patient's posture, gait, facial expression, grooming, dress, affect, gestures, speech, and thought content. However, relatively little time is spent on teaching the therapist trainee techniques for managing his or her own behavior. Fledgling therapists must pay particular attention to conforming to expected social mores regarding therapist behavior. With this in mind, the following are offered as tested techniques for use with patients.

Try to pay attention to what the patient is saying.

The patient is convinced that he or she brings a problem of importance to the therapy hour. He or she is also convinced that as a therapist, you will be keenly interested in this problem. One must give that impression. This is best achieved by listening to the patient. When it is not possible to listen, one must appear to be listening by the use of appropriate listening behaviors. These include eye contact (with the patient), animated facial expressions, posture gently inclined toward the patient, and periodic movement, such as nodding one's head. Asking a relevant question once in a while or offering a timely comment is generally seen as evidence that you are listening.

64

If you haven't been listening, learn to recover gracefully.

The idea is to demonstrate to the patient that although you may not have heard a word so far, you remain intensely interested. For example, "You are describing a complex situation, and I'm not quite following all the nuances of your story. Would you go over that last bit again?" If you remain clueless following this ploy, redirect the patient to a new subject with a transitional comment such as, "Yes, but how does this relate to your relationship with your mother?" This gives you another chance to pay attention. If what the patient was saying before was really important, he or she will get back to it.

Maintain alertness by diversion tactics.

If you're having an off day, visual imagery can help you maintain focus. As the patient describes various relationships and the aspects of inner life, try to visualize the persons and scenes. If these images are too distracting or difficult, associate to metaphors from fiction. For example, try to imagine which alien on Star Trek has the most features in common with your patient. This can suggest new lines of content to explore in terms of ego defenses. And some of those aliens are really attractive! Then try to imagine which alien you would most like to be stranded with on a shuttle that's lost navigational control. . . . Oops! Back to the patient.

Take notes.

Taking notes helps you to listen and stay focused on the patient. Discrete note taking persuades most patients that you are professional and that you care about getting their story straight. It also convinces managed care companies and peer reviewers that you are professional and a good liability risk. Keep a separate notepad next to the notepad of record for those special items that you may choose not to keep as part of the permanent patient record. An example of this side-by-side note taking is illustrated in Figure 1.

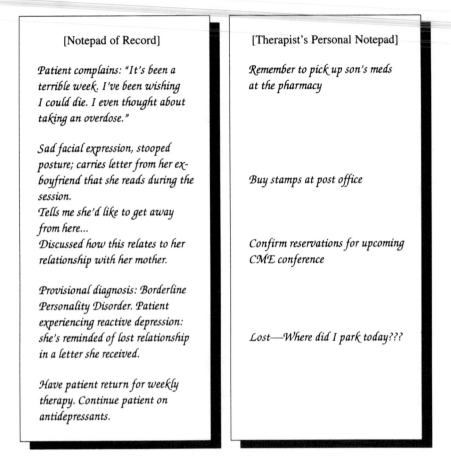

Figure 1. Sample of side-by-side note taking involving the notepad of record and the therapist's personal notepad.

Find something to do with your hands.

Patients generally react tactfully, but have difficulty engaging in a therapeutic alliance when therapists unravel the hems of their trousers during sessions. Note taking is useful to keep one's hands busy, but constant note taking can be an impediment to good therapy. The following techniques are suggested for therapists who fidget.

Paper clip tricks. Paper clips may be manipulated with one hand, or passed thoughtfully from hand to hand. During tense moments, paper clips can be bent back and forth several times. Paper clips that break during these manipulations should be discarded, as they can cause nasty cuts and bleeding. One should avoid making paper clip chains when in the presence of adult patients. And don't put them in your mouth.

Stapler tricks should be avoided. Staplers jam too easily and trying to get them unjammed is likely to be distracting to the patient.

Rubber band tricks. Rubber bands can be twisted thoughtfully in the fingers. Rubber bands can also be used as a mildly aversive stimuli to modify one's inattentive behaviors. A rubber band is worn on the wrist and snapped when one finds one's attention wandering. Avoid screaming "ouch!" as it will distract the patient from his or her own content during the therapy hour.

Office chairs. You finally got one of those great chairs that spins and rolls on casters! If you are especially fidgety, be honest about whether you can maintain eye contact while seated in a chair that has the capacity to spin and roll. If you can't maintain eye contact, switch chairs with your patient.

Conclusions

I really think Trills are the best aliens the Star Trek writers ever came up with. I mean, you can put male souls in gorgeous female bodies. And the car is in the south lot.

Curing a Phobia

Art Buchwald

One of the things that General Curtis LeMay said at a recent press conference was that Americans seem to have a phobia about nuclear weapons. This struck home because I have to admit I've had such a phobia for some time. But only after General LeMay brought it up did I decide to do something about it. I went to see Dr. Adolph Strainedluff, a psychiatrist who specializes in nuclear weapons phobias.

"On the couch," he said. "Vat seems to be the trouble?"

"Doctor," I said staring at the ceiling, "I have this fear of nuclear weapons. I know it's silly, but to me it's very real."

"Aha, very hinteresting. Ven did you first become aware of such a phobia?"

"I think it was around the time of Hiroshima or Nagasaki, I'm not sure which. I saw these photos of all these people killed and miles and miles of rubble, and suddenly I got this thing about atomic weapons."

Dr. Strainedluff tapped a pencil against his knee. "So tell me, how does this phobia manifest itself?"

"In peculiar ways, Doctor. I get the feeling if I ever see a mushroom cloud, I'm going to die."

"Very hinteresting, very hinteresting. You know it's all in the mind, don't you?"

"Of course. That's why I came to you. I don't want to do anything stupid."

Dr. Strainedluff said, "You are a very sick man. You think that just because an atomic bomb killed a few thousand people more than twenty years ago, you are threatened. You are manifesting infantile repressed hostility toward the weapons of war. In psychiatry we call this a military-industrial inferiority complex."

"I know I'm sick. You've got to help me," I begged.

"All right. First, you haff to get over this absurd fear of nuclear bombs. You must think of them as just another weapon in our vast defensive arsenal. Ve haff bowie knives and H-bombs, and in war, one is just as good as another. You're not afraid of a knife, are you?"

"Well, I don't think about it a lot."

"So, vhy should you be afraid of an H-bomb? It's another form of a knife."

"I never thought of it like that."

"Okay, so now let's look at some facts straight in the eye. In Bikini we blew up twenty bombs in an experiment. So ve thought everything vould be destroyed; that's how stupid ve were. Do you know that now after all the boom-boom, the place is flourishing and the rats are fatter than they ever vas before?"

"It's good to hear."

"The coconuts are hanging from the trees, the fish are svimming in the lagoon, and the voice of the turtle can be heard in the land. The only things that don't seem to be doing so good are the land crabs."

"I don't like land crabs," I said.

"So then you don't haff anything to vorry about."

Dr. Strainedluff started playing with the hand grenade which was attached to his watch fob. "If you're going to be a happy, normal human being," he shouted, "you're going to haff to stop with all these guilty peace feelings."

He was stomping around the room. "So get out of here vith your lousy phobias and all this stuff about being afraid to die. If you're not villing to take a little fallout for the good of the country, then go back vhere you came from!"

In spite of Dr. Strainedluff's final outburst, he did cure me of my phobia. I'm no longer afraid of nuclear weapons. Now I'm afraid of him.

Demystification of an Archetypal Symbol: Truth is Where You Find It

Albert D. Smouse, Ph.D.
University of Oklahoma

Many thinkers on the contemporary scene are familiar with the Jungian notion that certain symbols have the capacity to temporarily take on, embody, and convey universal truths (DeLaszlo, 1959), only to have their meaning fade over time. Once in a great while, however, a symbol is so powerful that it reemerges in its primitive form. Just such a case is exemplified by a message increasingly seen on the bumpers of pick-up trucks in the Southwestern United States. The symbol in its purest verbal form is "Shit Happens."

The demystification and explication of that symbol in order to restore its original richness of meaning represents a substantial contribution to the field. The methodology took a quantum leap forward when a review of the bulletin board literature revealed the data outlined in Table 1. This presentation stimulated the writer to take a parallel approach within the field of counseling psychology. Following a thorough search of the counseling psychology literature, a period of intense analysis produced the results shown in Table 2.

Table 1. Spiritual Truths

Source	Manifest Expression
Taoism	Shit happens.
Confucianism	Confucius say, "Shit happens."
Buddhism	If shit happens, it really isn't shit.
Hinduism	This shit happened before.
Islam	If shit happens, it is the will of Allah.
Protestantism	Shit happens to other people.
Catholicism	If shit happens, you deserve it.
Agnosticism	I won't believe this shit unless I see it.
Atheism	I don't believe this shit.
Judaism	Why does shit always happen to us?
Southern Baptist	You go to Hell for saying "Shit."
Jehovah's Witness	Let me into your house and I'll tell you why shit happens.
Alcoholics Anonymous	I trust in my higher power and can accept when shit happens.

Table 2. Psychotherapeutic Truths

Source	Manifest Expression
Reality Therapy	Shit happens.
Psychoanalysis	Shit happens during the anal stage.
Gestalt	You must get your shit together now.
Object Relations	How does it feel to shit on me?
Rogerian	You say "Feces occurs"?
Behavioral	Shit happening is reinforcing.
Rational Emotive	It is not logical to say "Woe is me" when shit happens.
Logotherapy	One is always free to shit.
Existential	Mankind must create meaning when shit happens.
Systems Approach	Stink is the negative feedback when shit happens.
Supportive Therapy	You shit well!
Organismic	Shit happens throughout the biosphere.
Humanistic	How do you feel about shit?
Eclectic	All kinds of shit happens.

References

DeLaszlo, V. (Ed.). (1959). *The basic writings of C. G. Jung.* New York: Random House.

Psychoproctology:
A New Clinical Specialty

Mark L. Pantle, Ph.D.
*A Major Southwest University that Wishes to
Remain Anonymous*

The field of clinical psychology has been distending at a rapid rate, and practitioners are feeling increased pressure (some would even say "urge") to answer the call of specialization. A variety of specialties has been brought forth in recent years (e.g., neuropsychology, forensic psychology, administrative psychology), prompting some to opine that the generalist in clinical psychology is in danger of being wiped away (Brann & Prune, 1989). Although those dedicated to the generalist model have expressed distress at its passing (e.g., Magnesia, 1990), others have breathed a sigh of relief (Lax, 1990).

Despite the development of numerous specialties in clinical psychology, none has yet emerged that addresses the essence, and angst, of our age. The transformations of hippies to yuppies, protestors into stockbrokers, and VWs into BMWs have driven Freud (1987) to label our era "The Anal Retentive Age." Citing cultural evidence to support his notion, he stated, "It is no coincidence that the two most obsessively coveted cars of our time, the BMW and the Mercedes Benz, both have the initials 'BM' " (p. 214).

Obviously, what is needed is a clinical specialty that is relevant to the Anal Retentive Age. Such a specialty requires a new perspective on our lives and on our selves; indeed, it demands that we turn the focus of psychology upside down. This article introduces this specialty for our time: Psychoproctology.

The theoretical underpinnings for Psychoproctology are found in Freud's early, previously undiscovered, and as yet untranslated works (1878).[1] As a poor student suffering from encopresis, Freud determined that the primary difference between him and the rich and successful, yet neurotic, people of Viennese society was that they had been successfully toilet trained. He abandoned the development of this theory after Charcot resolved his encopresis with hypnosis; however, the theory continued to color his later work. Indeed, the influence of his early formulation is evident in the name he gave his final product: psycho*anal*ysis.

In contrast to other aspects of Freudian theory, the relationship between success in toilet training and success in society has been empirically supported. In a study of the CEOs of Fortune 500 companies (Douglas & Sheen, 1987), a .89 correlation was found between salary and bowel control. It also found that these CEOs derived much pleasure from the pressures associated with the accumulation of material. However, such successful executives have been assessed as prone to dramatic mood swings (Dow & Jones, 1929, 1987) and other problems in living (Boesky & Keating, 1990).

The therapeutic goal of Psychoproctology is, very simply, to help clients "loosen up" by replacing the problems and pressures of material accumulation with the pride and pleasures of producing something that comes from deep within the self. The primary technique associated with the theory is Psychosuppository, which is alphabetically closer to psychotherapy than psychoanalysis. Psychosuppository is a short-term treatment technique, and significant therapeutic movement can occur within the first few sessions. Development of an implosive technique, labelled Emotional Enema, is currently underway.

Testimonials from clients treated with Psychosuppository have been flooding the offices of the Psychoproctology Institute. Here are just a few samples: "I discovered that I was flushing my life down the toilet. Now I know that life is not *a* waste—life *is* waste!" "Psychosuppository has given me a warm and wonderful feeling that

---

[1] Written on a yellow legal pad in ballpoint pen, this material was purchased from a reputable antique dealer in North Dakota, who assured me that it was authentic.

I haven't experienced in years." "I felt like a rat, man, until I got things worked out through Psychoproctology."

Every new therapeutic movement has its detractors, however, and Psychoproctology is no exception. Acknowledging the power of Psychosuppository as a treatment technique, Klisma and Fee-Lea (1991) have warned that clients may become addicted to therapy. Others have conducted a smear campaign against Psychoproctology, claiming that it threatens order and productivity in the workplace (O'Cee, 1991).

As a means of establishing itself as a viable and visible specialty, Psychoproctology will soon be announcing its Diplomate. The Diplomate, awarded by the Professional Organization Of Psychoproctology (P.O.O.P), will be printed on fine quality, two-ply paper and will be suitable for framing. The requirements for attaining the Diplomate will be attendance at a Psychoproctology Workshop and payment of requisite fees. Indeed, the process of paying the fees is itself considered a demonstration of commitment to the principles of Psychoproctology.

The downward displacement of psychology as proposed by Psychoproctology represents a radical shift in clinical theory and practice. Although some will welcome this new movement, others are likely to respond with upturned, or even plugged, noses. What does the future hold for Psychoproctology? We'll just have to wait to see how it comes out.

References

Boesky, I., & Keating, C. (1990). Mama said there'd be days like this. *Journal of Comparatively Constipated Psychology, 7,* 3–12.

Brann, O., & Prune, P. (1989). Cleaning up our act: The profusion of specialities in psychology. *Journal of Insulting and Cynical Psychology, 57,* 118–135.

Douglas, M., & Sheen, C. (1987). The boardroom is not a bathroom. *Quarterly Journal of the Study of the Sphincter, 51,* 20–27.

Dow, B., & Jones, B. (1929). Uh-oh. *Journal of Incontinent Economics, 10,* 105–113.

Dow, B., & Jones, B. (1987). The effects of junk food on mood. *Journal of Nutritional Economics, 3,* 82–87.

Freud, I. (1987). Things my great granduncle probably would say if he were alive today. *Journal of Nepotistic Psychology, 41,* 210–216.

Freud, S. (1878). *Dear diary.* Unpublished manuscript.

Klisma, A., & Fee-Lea, C. (1991). When therapy feels too good. *Journal of Addictions to Everything, 10,* 64–67.

Lax, X. (1990). It feels good to say goodbye: A response to Magnesia. *Annals of Banality, 81,* 57–58.

Magnesia, M. O. (1990). It hurts to say goodbye. *Annals of Banality, 81,* 54–56.

O'Cee, I. M. (1991). Nobody ever invented anything in a lavatory. *Journal of Grim and Humorless Psychology, 13,* 21–31.

3
Psychoanalysis

The Specimen

Deborah Hayden, M.A.

"Join us," she said. "We were just talking about how all of us at this table are currently seeing therapists."

He sat down. The dark-haired woman next to him interrupted her conversation to see who had joined them.

Using his tidbit of insider information he leaned a bit closer to her and said, "So, you're in analysis?"

"What do you mean by that?"

"It was just a friendly question."

"You always sit down next to a complete stranger and say 'So, urine analysis'?"

"Let's start over again. Do you have a therapist?"

"Of course, I have a therapist. I need a therapist to help me with fools like you who make fun of my job."

"Your job?"

"I analyze pee, o.k.? My friends didn't tell you?"

"Oh, of course. You're an analyst."

"Well, not really an analyst, more of a technician really."

"And you analyze 'P'. Who's 'P'?"

"Anybody's pee, for God's sake. Do you think I ask? Do you think I care? All the pees just get a number. Who are you anyway? My therapist thinks I should change jobs. He thinks people laugh at us."

"He should know of course. Do you ever analyze yourself?"

"Why, do I look sick?"

"You look fine, but you are a little touchy. Tell me, don't you think it's a little impersonal to use numbers for people?"

79

"Of course not. It's called confidentiality."

"But how can you talk to them if you don't even know their names?"

"Listen, I analyze them, o.k., I don't talk to them. I mean I don't have conversations with them or something. I scan to find out if they have something to diagnose, so they can get the right drugs. For most things, we give them the right drugs, and zip! We never see them again. You think I spend my whole day talking? You think talking to them would make any difference? You're the type who talks to your plants."

"You're the type who says 'um' a lot and get paid gobs by the hour."

"I get paid shit and if you make a joke about that I'll throw something at you."

"Aren't you people supposed to work out your hostilities before you get to work with your so-called 'P's'?"

"Maybe a little natural hostility keeps me from connecting the numbers with the sick people behind them."

"I've heard about medicine without a soul, but you are really the limit."

"Look, I come in to work in the morning, I put on a white coat, and in front of me are not people but biological specimens. You want me to call them by name? You want me to say, yo, Marvin, you're looking a little pale today?"

"Marvin might appreciate it."

"Marvin is nobody to me, do you get it? Nobody is Marvin."

"How can Marvin feel like somebody if you treat him like a jar of urine?"

"What do you want here? You would rather Marvin comes in and pees on my desk for me? Is that what you want, you lunatic?"

"Marvin might not feel like peeing on your desk if you treated him like a human being."

"Great. Maybe I could ask him how he feels about his mother and then he wouldn't pee on my desk."

"Maybe not."

"Fine. Then how would I get him to pee on my desk?"

"Why would you want him to pee on your desk?"

"Marvin doesn't pee on my desk, I don't get paid. Am I having this conversation?"

"I think the health care system needs to be overhauled."

"I think you need to be overhauled."

"One thing is sure. I'm never going to become a 'P' of yours."

"Well, you never know now do you? You might get lucky."

New Horizons in Psychoanalysis: Treatment of Necrosistic Personality Disorders

Don R. Swanson, Ph.D.
University of Chicago

Whether the insights of psychoanalysis can be used to cast light on historically important activities of people long dead is a matter of spirited dispute among scholars (Freud, 1957; Stannard, 1980). The disputants seem to be singularly uninterested, however, in whether such insights might benefit the patients themselves. Insensitivity of this kind is only part of a larger pattern of discrimination against the dead. Grave inequities are revealed by a few lethal statistics. Of the 60 billion people on earth, over 90 percent are dead. Yet nearly everyone in treatment for a mental or emotional disorder is alive. So great a disparity invites suspicion that the dead do not have equal opportunity for help. Resources are not lacking; surely in a country where even the national product is gross, more can be done.

Origins of Necroanalysis

The foundation for a clinically based theory of necrosism has been in place for over a century. The origin of this work can be credited to the generally excellent care, attention, and treatment that dead patients receive in medical schools and teaching hospitals, even though elsewhere they are discarded and ignored. In the summer of 1883, at the General Hospital in Vienna, a brilliant young resident in psychiatry, Floyd Siegman, first began to wonder why face-to-face therapy consistently failed with these patients. The immediate problem seemed to center on their inability to remain upright for the required 50-minute session. Floyd could not escape the compelling idea that the dead have an affinity for the horizontal. He observed, too, that they are prone to remain silent for long periods of time. These two principles—silence and horizontalness—were destined to become the headstones for a revolutionary approach to psychotherapy, an approach that offers new hope for the dead. Dr. Einar Kleine Schwanstücker, a noted Viennese necroanalyst, recently unearthed heretofore unknown correspondence between Floyd and his friend Felice (Swanson, 1977, pp. 137–153), letters that encapsulate the body of this new theory and provide dramatic evidence from two case histories, outlined herewith, that death can be understood and successfully treated as a necrosistic personality disorder.

Case 1: Leda

Leda, an attractive woman, 26, single, and the youngest in a large family, sought help a few years after her death. She complained that death held no meaning, that she lacked spirit, felt stiff, and often thought she might be better off alive. Unable to accept the loss of her living companions, Leda frequently attempted to join them. Her friends, unreceptive to these overtures, fled in panic whenever she materialized in their presence. Leda was mortified. She took to lying around Central Park at night and had a series of brief encounters with occasional necrophilic passers-by. These adventures brought little genuine satisfaction. Men thought she was cold. When finally someone took her home, Leda was hopeful that a more enduring relationship might develop, but the authorities soon discovered the liaison and intervened. This event precipitated Leda's initial visit to a necroanalyst, Dr. Einar Grosser Schwanstücker.

The analyst correctly perceived Leda's pathology in terms of a failure to mourn her self. Loss of the self, as object, brings about an introjection of the object, as self. Working-through of hostility toward the introjected self-object is prerequisite to mourning. The eventual decathexis and extrojection of the self-object and the object-self are appropriate therapeutic aims and lead finally to mature acceptance of death. After 2 years of analytic work, the patient learned to extroject introjects by turning her insights out. The analysis then progressed rapidly. By the time of termination, Leda was virtually free of her crippling zest for life and made no further attempts to commit animation. She abandoned her haunts in Central Park and moved to Chicago. The opportunity for employment by the city, and being encouraged to vote, helped her for the first time since she died to feel valued. A few months later Leda married a respectable young cadaver just out of medical school.

Case 2: Tut-tut

Our second case brings to light quite different aspects of necrosism. The analysis was conducted by a candidate who was supervised.

Tut-tut, an illegitimate son of King Tut, peacefully interred for 3,000 years, sought treatment following a traumatic encounter with an archaeologist. The patient, completely unraveled, had been placed on display in a museum. Helping Tut-tut manage the resulting over-stimulation of his exhibitionistic tendencies quickly became the focal problem of the analysis. Within a year the patient's fantasies had become organized around a conviction that the analyst, too, was dead—fantasies that clearly pointed to a mummy transference. The treatment was characterized by absolute silence, unbroken for 3 years by either patient or analyst. A certain ineffable quality in the silence aroused the suspicion of the supervisor who, on investigating, found that the analyst had in fact died 2 years earlier. Owing to countertransference difficulties, he had been unaware of his own death.

Analysts more concerned with content than process might have seen at this point a crisis calling for abrupt termination of the analysis. The supervisor, however, had the presence of mind to recall that the candidate needed only 60 more hours with this patient to fulfill all requirements for certification, and so perceived that immediate termination would be detrimental to the analytic process. The wisdom of allowing the analysis to continue was underscored by subsequent events. Termination material soon appeared spontaneously. The patient became more comfortable with his position at the museum. He gave up exhibiting spectacular resurrections and was finally able to enjoy being admired for his authentic, eternal qualities. Relations with co-workers and supervisors improved. Opportunities for advancement presented themselves. He was given greater responsibility and transferred to a larger, better-lighted showcase.

The case of Tut-tut illuminates important issues of analytic silence, empathy, and certain matters of life and death that have far-reaching implications.

Silence, Transference, and Empathy

It is commonly believed that a live analyst is preferable to a dead one. There is no evidence to support this idea. Such a view, indeed, reflects serious misunderstanding of the analytic process, not to say a failure to distinguish the temporal from the eternal. What really matters is the unfolding and management of the transference. Thousands of patients have been treated successfully with dead analysts. This fact tends not to be widely known, for nearly all patients believe, under the influence of the transference and in the face of clear evidence to the contrary, that their own analyst is alive. While it is not strictly necessary that an analyst be dead, there are several advantages. Few living analysts are able to appreciate the basic fact that all interventions are irrelevant, and that a single fundamental rule governs all successful treatment—a simple categorical imperative: *The analyst shouldn't mix in.*

Some analysts have warned nevertheless that regression induced in patients by complete silence can be fatal. That may be so, but the demise of the patient is not to be taken as an unfavorable prognostic sign. Death in the service of the ego is almost always an encouraging therapeutic development. Patients who cannot tolerate lengthy analytic silences before they die do so remarkably well afterward.

To understand how dead silence can be helpful, one must first understand what is meant by silence. Analytic silence should not be confused with ordinary silence. Analytic silence is entirely different. It is fraught with empathy. The progress of an analysis can in fact be measured by the flow of empathy (or possibly entropy [Swanson, 1977a, 1977b]) from the analyst to the patient. This flow is called transference. If the empathy is too thick to flow, it can be fed by spoon. The termination phase begins when the patient is fed up.

Future Directions

Our future work on necrosism will focus on the identification and classification of its various types of transference. We have provisionally divided these necrosistic transferences into four groups—transcendental, ectoplasmic, ecumenical, and apocalyptic—categories that, we now have reason to think, may give birth to the recognition that "death, the most exalted object we are capable of conceiving" (C. Darwin, private communication) may take on a rich variety of forms.

References

Freud, S. (1957). Leonardo da Vinci and a memory of his childhood. In *The standard edition of the complete works of Sigmund Freud* (Vol. 11, pp. 63–137). London: Hogarth Press. (Original work published 1910)

Stannard, D. (1980). *Shrinking history: On Freud and the failure of psychohistory.* Oxford: Oxford University Press.

Swanson, D. R. (1977a). On force, energy, entropy, and the assumptions of metapsychology. In T. Shapiro (Ed.), *Psychoanalysis and contemporary science* (Vol. 5). New York: International University Press.

Swanson, D. R. (1977b). Critique of psychic energy as an explanatory concept. *Journal of the American Psychoanalytic Association, 25,* 603–633.

California Dreamin'

Lee Israel

The following is one in a series of analyses by Sigmund Freud of dreams he dreamt in the early spring of 1903. *"Der kalifornische Traum"* (California Dreamin') is published here for the first time.

The dream.   I dream that I am riding horseback on a wide road somewhere in the western American state of California. At my side is a disgraced, fugitive Negro sports figure, once held in the highest regard in the hearts of the world, suspected now of having murdered most brutally his beautiful former wife and also a young man who arrived unfortunately at the killing site whilst returning a pair of spectacles. The fallen hero rides a large, white bucking horse and threatens from time to time to kill himself. I am calling him the Juice. I am imploring him not to kill himself, saying, "Don't give up, Juice. The Dream Team (*die Gangentraum*) will set you free." Meanwhile, we are all the time being chased by a massive constabulary, but they and we move at a slow, almost balletic tempo—quite surreal and typical of the altered dream state. There are flickering lights everywhere. We are plainly the focus of a hovering, tremendous attention: all eyes are upon the Juice and me.

I am awaking with a full bladder, but not before Little Hans, a patient of yore, rides up beside me and addresses me with a galling familiarity. "Let's see you free-associate your way out of this one, Pops," he says, flashing a Tarot card at me. "You've just prophesied the trial of the century!"

Dream analysis.   In the dream, I am on horseback throughout—
and indeed the horse motif infuses the entire manifest content. As
a matter of fact, I cannot ride and would not dream of doing so,
although the equestrian theme is not uncommon in my sleeping
thoughts. Some years ago, for instance, I had a boil in my scrotal
area; so painful was the boil that it inspired a dream in which I also
rode on the back of a horse precisely because the act of equitation
was so contraindicated, would have been such pure *meshugga,* that
doing so was like wishing away the boil. I was saying to myself,
"Freud, you couldn't possibly have a suppurating lump of disease
on your perineum the size of a small cabbage because you are riding
a horse!" Now on the day previous to the present dream about
the fallen American sports figure, I ran into a lecturer at Vienna
University whom we'll call Doctor Ü. (not his real initial)—a man
whose recent monograph on plant biology impressed me greatly.
After complementing him appropriately, I inquired as to whether
he had yet seen the new Schnitzler play at the Ring Theater. Ü.
rejoined, "Wild horses couldn't drag me thither! (*Keine zehn Pferde
bringen mich dahin.*") I experienced great resentment at the tone
taken by Ü., at the haughtiness with which he had dismissed my
distinguished friend Schnitzler and by extension me. I even con-
sciously wished him a suppurating boil on his testicle that would drive
him to dreams of riding horses. But my conscious ill-disposedness
apparently was not nasty enough because I had so plainly represented
him in the dream as the dark, disgraced fugitive. This became more
obvious as I brought to my conscious thoughts the recollected knowledge that Doctor Ü., in his salad days, had been a remarkably talented
sculler, thrice winner of the Kaiser Wilhelm Pole Vault medal (the
"Villie"). And also Ü. was married happily to a very beautiful
woman, Frau Ü.: the apple of his eye. Frau Ü., it happens, is outstand-
ingly endowed: a Rubenesque, bosomy, one might even say *saft* or
saftig little lady. Here the dream-work practically calls out to me,
"Yoo-hoo, Freud!" Of course, *saft* translates to juice, the English
word I am calling him in the dream. Bingo! By a process of displacement I am wreaking terrible vengeance on Ü. by placing him in
harm's way, an utterly disgraced uxoricide, having murdered most
brutally the great love of his life, the ample apple: Frau Ü.

   But just as I am about to put on my hat and take an afternoon's

stroll about Vienna it comes to me that there might be some pro-
foundly non-Ü. material with which I have not yet dealt. My thoughts
pass immediately to the cameo appearance in my sleeping script of
the erstwhile patient, Hans. As anyone who has read my previous
work will by this time know, Little Hans was a mere stripling when
his crippling phobias, particularly his fear of leaving the house because he might be bitten by a horse, were brought on by his Mama
who had come upon him in the act of self-gratification and warned
him, "Keep it up, Hansel, and the doctor will make here a visit and
turn you into Gretel." The horses subsequently feared by Hans lest
they bite off his already tiny wienie represented, naturally, the Papa
(English: "hung like a horse," in *The Dictionary of Dirt and Filth*
[*Die Enzkopadie mit Schmutzigkeit und Dreck*]). After I helped
liberate Hans from his castration complex by persuading him that
he should fear neither horses nor Papa, but rather Mama, the little
guy left the house as often as possible, and also became a great
admirer of my work, particularly the theory of the dream as the
royal way to the nettlesome Unconscious. How comes it then that
he invades my dream flashing the Tarot card, preaching the pharaonic
doctrine of the dream as future predictor? I had begun to think of
Little Hans as my "pupil"; and now as I examine anew the material
of the dream, I see him as my seditious, talkative, and "dilating
pupil," an embarrassingly obvious reference to the expansion of the
eye under the influence of a drug. His evocation of this "trial of the
century" becomes my own titanic struggle with the decidedly mixed
blessing of *Erthroxylon coca,* cocaine, under the influence of which
I had been best and brightest, animated in work and in life with
the most gorgeous excitement, exhilaration, and euphoria. Could
anything be clearer than the meaning of the young man carrying the
eyeglasses and dying for this venture, this "trip"? The spectacles
symbolize the enhancement, the insight bestowed by the miraculous,
but alas also murderous, cocaine. (German: *Brille* = eyeglasses, but
klosett Brille = toilet seat. See also, in Lewis Carroll's obviously
drug-induced poem, *Jabberwocky* [German: *Yabbervocky*], "T'was
brillig, and the slithy toves . . ." [emphasis added].) I see now, of
course, that the white bucking horse, the Bronco, stands for my
desire still for the rambunctious, unmanageable highs (the high
horse = *hohe Pferde*) of the old days before I became aware of the

addicting, pernicious effects: the ca-ca of coca; the constabulary becomes hence my own reining-in prudence. But in the dream, and in many dreams, I am wishing still for the paradisal potency of the white horse: my *lieblich Kokain*. I have tamed the beastly botanical but the wish persists.

And now I can put on my hat?

4
Clinical Case Studies

A Profile of Politically Correct Interpersonal Relating: The Case of Little Red Riding Hood

James Finn Garner

There once was a young person named Red Riding Hood who lived with her mother on the edge of a large wood. One day her mother asked her to take a basket of fresh fruit and mineral water to her grandmother's house—not because this was womyn's work, mind you, but because the deed was generous and helped engender a feeling of community. Furthermore, her grandmother was *not* sick, but rather was in full physical and mental health and was fully capable of taking care of herself as a mature adult.

So Red Riding Hood set off with her basket through the woods. Many people believed that the forest was a foreboding and dangerous place and never set foot in it. Red Riding Hood, however, was confident enough in her own budding sexuality that such obvious Freudian imagery did not intimidate her.

On the way to Grandma's house, Red Riding Hood was accosted by a wolf, who asked her what was in her basket. She replied, "Some healthful snacks for my grandmother, who is certainly capable of taking care of herself as a mature adult."

The wolf said, "You know, my dear, it isn't safe for a little girl to walk through these woods alone."

Red Riding Hood said, "I find your sexist remark offensive in the extreme, but I will ignore it because of your traditional status as an outcast from society, the stress of which has caused you to develop your own, entirely valid, worldview. Now, if you'll excuse me, I must be on my way."

Red Riding Hood walked on along the main path. But, because his status outside society had freed him from slavish adherence to linear, Western-style thought, the wolf knew a quicker route to Grandma's house. He burst into the house and ate Grandma, an entirely valid course of action for a carnivore such as himself. Then, unhampered by rigid, traditionalist notions of what was masculine and feminine, he put on Grandma's nightclothes and crawled into bed.

Red Riding Hood entered the cottage and said, "Grandma, I have brought you some fat-free, sodium-free snacks to salute you in your role of a wise and nurturing matriarch."

From the bed, the wolf said softly, "Come closer, child, so that I might see you."

Red Riding Hood said, "Oh, I forgot you are as optically challenged as a bat. Grandma, what big eyes you have!"

"They have seen much, and forgiven much, my dear."

"Grandma, what a big nose you have—only relatively, of course, and certainly attractive in its own way."

"It has smelled much, and forgiven much, my dear."

"Grandma, what big teeth you have!"

The wolf said, "I am happy with *who* I am and *what* I am," and leaped out of bed. He grabbed Red Riding Hood in his claws, intent on devouring her. Red Riding Hood screamed, not out of alarm at the wolf's apparent tendency toward cross-dressing, but because of his willful invasion of her personal space.

Her screams were heard by a passing woodchopper-person (or log-fuel technician, as he preferred to be called). When he burst into the cottage, he saw melee and tried to intervene. But as he raised his ax, Red Riding Hood and the wolf both stopped.

"And just what do you think you're doing?" asked Red Riding Hood.

The woodchopper-person blinked and tried to answer, but no words came to him.

"Bursting in here like a Neanderthal, trusting your weapon to do your thinking for you!" she exclaimed. "Sexist! Speciesist! How dare you assume that women and wolves can't solve their own problems without a man's help!"

When she heard Red Riding Hood's impassioned speech, Grandma jumped out of the wolf's mouth, seized the woodchopper-person's ax, and cut his head off. After this ordeal, Red Riding Hood, Grandma, and the wolf felt a certain commonality of purpose. They decided to set up an alternative household based on mutual respect and cooperation, and they lived together in the woods happily ever after.

5
Educational Psychology and Education

Communication Variance Patterns in Academic Employment Announcements

Mitchell M. Handelsman, Ph.D.
University of Colorado at Denver

Joseph J. Palladino, Ph.D.
University of Southern Indiana

As the hiring process becomes more competitive, litigious, obnoxious, and strenuous, we notice that advertisements for academic positions are becoming more difficult to understand. The reasons behind how job ads are worded vary: hiring practices, the ascendance of college and university risk management practices, budget cuts, etc. As a result of these various influences, ads for academic employment opportunities tend to be convoluted and deceptive. Our purpose here is simply to offer some examples of actual job descriptions published in recent issues of the *Chronicle of Higher Education,* along with the "between-the-lines" information they contain. By lowering the signal-to-noise ratio in these ads, we hope to enable people to make better informed decisions about the jobs for which they apply.

We first present employment ads as they appear in print. Each ad, or "phenotype," is then followed by the "genotype," which accurately reflects the real meaning of the information provided.

Academic Ad Phenotype	Academic Ad Genotype
". . . must be able to teach a variety of courses offered by the department."	. . . must be able to teach *all* of the courses offered by the department.

Academic Ad Phenotype	Academic Ad Genotype
". . . a high level of relevant business and accounting experience required."	The accountant tells us we're over budget, but we don't know how to read the computer printout.
". . . working knowledge of public schools."	. . . no chance for tenure; keep your teaching license current.
". . . seeks a head for a two-person department."	The funeral was last week, the arraignment is tomorrow.
". . . located in an area of scenic beauty."	No fringe benefits.
". . . a cohesive department."	No one was assaulted at the *last* department meeting.
". . . it has long been a cultural center of the arts."	Nearby Wal-Mart and Kmart both have excellent art reproductions.
". . . the position requires working closely with the faculty."	You'll share office space.
". . . lead collegially, consult readily, and delegate responsibly."	. . . buy donuts every Friday, don't make a move without checking with senior faculty, and dump committee assignments on junior faculty.

Academic Ad Phenotype	Academic Ad Genotype
". . . demonstrated teaching competence and academic background in human sexuality, undergraduate and master's degree in related fields with a strong background in human sexuality education."	Our enrollments are down significantly.
". . . the candidate must also develop program thrusts."	Hey, wasn't that part of the human sexuality ad?
"The university regards the southern Indiana region as a laboratory where many economic development and community partnership activities are underway."	We hear that they're going to reopen the bowling alley downtown.
". . . salaries may be enhanced by supplemental teaching."	. . . salaries may be lowered by the state legislature.
"The president must be socially adept and have the ability to communicate with and represent the institution to its outside constituencies."	Holy cow, do we need money!

Understanding Your Doctoral Students: A Guide for Beginning Professors

Alan Feingold, M.Phil.
Yale University

Recent articles (Feingold, 1990, 1992; Pierce, 1990) have addressed the discrepancies between what professors tell their graduate students and what they actually mean. However, professors do not have a monopoly on misrepresentation—just more experience. Professors must correctly interpret what their doctoral students say, and new professors who fail to do so risk losing their students. Then their research program falters, promotion is denied, and they're off to a non–tenure-track adjunct assistant professorship at Alabama State Community College. To aid the beginning professor, the author offers interpretations of frequent student comments and questions. Armed with such knowledge, the young academic having initial dealings with graduate students can better gauge exactly how much he or she can get away with.

What Your Doctoral Students Say	What Your Doctoral Students Mean
I'm really happy to be here.	All the other schools I applied to rejected me.
I became interested in social psychology after exposure to cognitive dissonance theory and recognizing its insight into counterintuitive results.	I became interested in social psychology because I couldn't get into a clinical psychology program, but I figured I could transfer later

102

What Your Doctoral Students Say	What Your Doctoral Students Mean
	once I proved my usefulness to the clinical faculty.
The curriculum is a bit more intense than I had expected.	Who developed the curriculum, the Marquis de Sade?
Are all these readings required?	Must I buy every book you've written?
Which faculty are good to work with?	Who calls the shots around here?
Of course I did the reading.	I just didn't understand a word of it.
How long does it take to complete the program?	How long must I suffer?
My participation in the instructional program of the college would broaden my knowledge of the discipline.	I could really use the money from teaching, no matter how pathetically little it may be.
Are statistical consultants available?	Can I find people to design my studies for me?
Is there an instructor's manual for the class I've been asked to teach?	Hey, I have more important things to do with my time than prepare lectures and write exam questions myself.
The results were ambiguous so the analyses must be rerun.	The analyses haven't been run yet.

What Your Doctoral Students Say	What Your Doctoral Students Mean
Although the results were contrary to those predicted based on *your* theory, I'm certain they were an artifact of my flawed operationalizations of the independent variables.	My lips are sealed.
I hope you're aware of all the time and work I'm putting into this project.	I am getting a co-authorship out of this, aren't I?
Now that I'm finally completing my Ph.D., I hope I can count on you for a solid letter of recommendation.	I hope I didn't spend six years sucking up to you for nothing.

References

Feingold, A. (1990). Understanding your advisor: A survivor's guide for beginning graduate students. *Journal of Polymorphous Perversity, 7*(1), 12–14.

Feingold, A. (1992). Understanding your advisor II: More survival tips for fledgling graduate students unfamiliar with "advisor-speak." *Journal of Polymorphous Perversity, 9*(1), 10–11.

Pierce, D. L. (1990). Understanding your doctoral dissertation committee: A survivor's guide for advanced graduate students. *Journal of Polymorphous Perversity, 7*(2), 19–20.

Understanding Your Advisor II: More Survival Tips for Fledgling Graduate Students Unfamiliar With Interpreting "Advisor-Speak"

Alan Feingold, M.Phil.
Yale University

In an earlier article, Feingold (1990) cautioned graduate students that there is a world of difference between what an academic advisor says and what he or she actually means, and he offered some interpretations of "advisor-speak" for new students. This article is a supplement to the earlier "survivor's guide," providing additional explanations of common advisor's comments. Moreover, it illustrates how understanding one's advisor is often not so much a matter of interpreting what is said, but of being able to fill in what is left unsaid.

What Your Advisor Says	What Your Advisor Means
Because we're a "helping profession," beginning students are often surprised that we provide an individualistic and nonnurturing environment.	Welcome to the psychology department from hell.
The faculty are competitive.	The faculty are ruthless.
The faculty are friendly but competitive.	The faculty are devious and ruthless.
The objective of the program is to educate scholars.	. . . in the sense that the objective of a commercial is to inform consumers.

What Your Advisor Says	What Your Advisor Means
Our undergraduate students get their B.S. upon leaving.	. . . in contrast to our graduate students, who get it upon arrival.
A good graduate student is flexible and sensitive to faculty feedback.	A good graduate student is easily controlled.
We don't treat students like dirt.	We try not to step on dirt.
It's helpful that you have a master's as well as a B.A.	We like to give our students the third degree.
Psychology is the world's most important science, and I am one of its greatest scholars, although my contributions are often belittled by envious colleagues.	I'm an asshole.
I'd like to help you but given the multitude of demands on my limited time . . .	What's in it for me?
Our clinical students gain valuable psychotherapy experience at the University Health Center.	Somebody's gotta listen to the problems of the undergraduates.
Judgments of the quality of student research are fair and objective.	If we like you, your research is great. If we don't, it sucks.
I may be wrong.	. . . but who the hell are you to challenge me?

What Your Advisor Says	What Your Advisor Means
I like students who disagree with me.	. . . when I say things like, "I may be wrong."
If you have a dispute with a professor, you can file a grievance with the Graduate School.	. . . but the administration always sides with the faculty.
If you have any problems, I'll always be there to give you a hand.	. . . but if helping you conflicts with my own interests, you'll only get the finger.
Graduate school grades aren't important when you are seeking a position.	. . . but a letter from your advisor is—so you'd better spend less time on your studies and more time on my research.
Most of our students get good jobs.	. . . assuming they have an enthusiastic letter from their advisor.
Congratulations, you're now a Ph.D.	I've gotten all I can from you. Now get the hell outta here.

References

Feingold, A. (1990). Understanding your advisor: A survivor's guide for beginning graduate students. *Journal of Polymorphous Perversity, 7*(1), 12–14.

Etal Tells All:
An Exclusive Interview With
the World's Most Prolific Scientist

Mike Dubik, M.D., and Brian Wood, M.D.
Eastern Virginia Medical School

As everyone knows, there is no more frequently referenced author in the sciences, arts, and humanities than Etal. Although often quoted, he is rarely seen outside his mythical ivory tower. Dr. Etal has granted us this rare and exclusive interview.

Dr. Etal, please tell us about yourself.
Only the shallow know themselves. (Wilde, O.)

Well, tell us about your beginnings.
It is popular today to say that we have found the child within us. For me, this would be a short search. (Cosby, B.) I was the kid next door's imaginary friend. (Phillips, E.)

Why have you avoided interviews until now?
I'm afraid of losing my obscurity. Genuineness only thrives in the dark. Like celery. (Huxley, A.)

Well, you're certainly quite a celebrity in academic circles.
The nice thing about being a celebrity is that, if you bore people, they think it's their fault. (Kissinger, H.)

We have noticed over the years that you are a senior investigator in innumerable articles in diverse areas of science, medicine, humanities, and the arts. We are intrigued and astounded by your productivity.

How do you explain your expertise in so many fields?
Do everything. One thing may turn out right. (Bogart, H.)

To our knowledge you are not the first author on any major research paper. Why?
I allow my junior colleagues to enjoy principal authorship. Besides, there are only two kinds of researchers: those who do the work and those who take the credit. I try to be in the first group; there is less competition. (Gandhi, I.)

What do you hope to accomplish as a research scientist?
I hope to obtain grant money, of course. After all, it is better to have a permanent income than to be fascinating. (Wilde, O.)

Have you ever had any bureaucratic hassles getting your work published?
If you're going to sin, sin against God, not the bureaucracy. God will forgive you but the bureaucracy won't. (Rickover, H. G.)

That almost sounds bitter, doctor.
Not really. I never attribute to malice that which is adequately explained by stupidity. (Hanlon)

We take it you have an opinion on government regulation of scientific research.
Indeed. I have found that when I work directly for the government I spend more and more time reporting on my work and less and less time actually working. On some projects I have achieved a steady state wherein I continually reported on work that is not getting done. (Anon)

Have you found the "publish or perish" world of academic research to be a rat race?
Yes, and even when you win, you're still a rat. (Tomlin, L.)

Do you enjoy your work?
I know it's dangerous to enjoy your work too much (Snoopy) but, for me, work is much more fun than fun. (Coward, N.)

Do you feel your work is important?
I have come to realize that an early symptom of approaching mental illness is the belief that one's work is terribly important. If you consider your work very important you should take a day off. (Russell, B.)

How do you get your ideas?
The best way to have a good idea is to have a lot of ideas. (Pauling, L.)

You don't seem to have slowed down at all over the years. How have you stayed so active?
You're never too old to do goofy stuff (Cleaver, W.). Besides, when you're over the hill, you begin to pick up speed. (Schulz, C.)

How has science academia changed over the years?
Just because things are different doesn't mean anything has changed. (Porter, I.)

That's an interesting judgment.
Good judgment comes from experience. Experience comes from bad judgment. (Anon)

You have been called one of the world's leading authorities on a wide variety of subjects.
Yes. As an expert I know tremendous amounts about very little. (Butler, N. M.)

We think it is fair to say that you are a heroic figure to scientists and researchers everywhere.
Maybe. But no one is a hero to his valet (Nietzsche, F. W.) or his spouse's psychiatrist. (Berne, E.)

Do you have any general advice for your fellow scientists?
Yes. When you have a lot to do, get your nap over with first. (Anderson, J.) Also, never play cat and mouse games if you're a mouse. (Dickson, P.) But, then again, no generalization is wholly true, not even this one. (Holmes, O. W.) Besides, no one wants advice—only corroboration. (Steinbeck, J.)

Do you have any words of encouragement to budding scientists?
Always look out for number one and be careful not to step in number two. (Dangerfield, R.)

You're a strong proponent of education?
Education is what survives when what has been learned has been forgotten. (Skinner, B. F.) So, I'm always ready to learn, though often I don't like being taught. (Churchill, W.)

So does everyone need to learn science?
One does not need to know science but he should at least have forgotten it. (Brander, M.)

Well then what is science all about?
The term science should not be given to anything but the aggregate of the recipes that are always successful. All the rest is literature. (Valery, P.)

Why did you choose science as a career?
I like simple things. My mother recognized this tendency in me early and when she heard that science is the art of systematic over-simplification (Popper, K.), she figured I was a natural.

You also teach?
Yes, and the hardest part has always been to keep the students awake. For every academic required to teach there are at least thirty reluctant students required to take the class, ready to be bored. (Sellar, W. C.)

What is the hardest subject you've taught?
Never try to teach a pig to sing. It wastes your time and annoys the pig. (Anon)

How was the pay as a teacher?
I was certainly overpaid as a teacher but I was ludicrously underpaid as a babysitter. (Osborne, J.)

Have you also served as an administrator?
Yes. At various institutions and everywhere I was confronted by the same three problems: sex and rock & roll for the students; sports for the alumni; and parking for the faculty. (Kerr, C.)

How do you balance being a scientist, teacher, and administrator?
Simple. On good days I'm a scientist; on not so good days, I teach; and on really bad days, when I can't teach, I administrate. (Shaw, G. B.)

What do researchers need to know these days?
It is better to know some of the questions than all the answers. (Thurber, J.)

Is there anyone to whom you owe your success?
I'm a self-made man, which shows what happens when you don't follow directions. (Hoest, B.)

As we wind up the interview, are there any other observations you would like to share?
Yes. If dandelions were hard to grow, they would be most welcome on any lawn. (Mason, A. V.) Eighty percent of life is just showing up. (Allen, W.) Oh, yes, and spend the afternoon, you can't take it with you. (Dillard, A.)

What are your research interests now?
I'd like to know how a committee can make a decision dumber than any of its members. (Coblitz, D. B.) I'd like to know why life can't present all its problems when you're 17 and know all the answers. (Jolly, A. C.)

One last question. What does it all mean, Dr. Etal?
I don't know, I don't care, and it doesn't make any difference. (Kerouac, J.)

So, what's the answer doctor?
There ain't no answer. There ain't going to be any answer. There never has been an answer. That's the answer. (Stein, G.)

We tend to agree.

Well then, if we are in complete agreement then I propose we postpone further interviewing to give ourselves time to develop disagreement and perhaps gain some understanding and insight into what we are talking about. (Sloan, A. P.)

Basic Concepts in the Behavioral Sciences: What I Learned in Psychology 101

Jamie Martindale, M.S.

Several researchers (Mischel, 1977; Vaughan, 1977) in the field of psychology have investigated the degree to which untrained members of the general public can use common sense to understand general principles of psychology. However, not yet studied in depth is the phenomenon of the leap in understanding that typically occurs after one's first course in introductory psychology. Along these lines, therefore, the following set of randomly selected data from exams, journals, and projects is offered as a starting point for this investigation. May these fragments—all direct quotes—help us piece together the puzzle of what is truly learned in psychology.

Items of Historical Significance

Pavlov studied the salvation of a dog. Food causes the salvation.

Erikson created the identity crisis for teenagers and the mid-life crisis for middle-aged people.

Freud's stages were oral, anal, phallic, lunatic, and gentle.

Key Scientific Facts

His studies were sexiest, and he tended to use control groups of people that weren't very large.

114

Constant reinforcement is easier to break than partical reinforcement.

Adopted by different families, they grew 45 miles apart in Ohio.

Learning about Abnormal Behavior

Bulimia is also called the binge-plunge syndrome.

I would look for symptoms like if he were having delusions, hallucinations, or being non-commutive.

What do you think about these others with fetishes and these transtesticles, or whatever?

C.P. is a condition in which interference with the control of motor systems arise as a result of liaisons occurring from birth trauma.

Understanding Human Development

Infants develop their lounge skills and try them out by imitating brothers and sisters.

During the toddler stag you mimik what others say and do.

They gain abilities like climbing, walking, and keeping balances.

They learn by trail and eror.

He was weaker in things like math and other classes where he is required to read and conceive.

Appreciation of Cultural Differences

Some cults even encourage members to kill people, such as Hare Krishnas.

One of the main things I learned in this class was not to be prejuiced.

These people are not censored from fowl language.

I was amazed at the whinos, & the prostitutes with their costumers.

They have learned to give the dolphins an award after a trick.

Insight into the Behavior of Others

My mother is more of a mixed-brain.

Scott enjoys being around people and making new ones all the time.

Many believed their dreams reviled things about their future.

My Uncle, for example, died of cancer a few years ago, and he took it pretty well at first.

He stands out like a sour thumb.

Mary was taken to a suicidal prevention center.

He really went for the juggler.

Enhanced Self-Awareness

My goal in class is to learn to get alone with everyone.

I want to do well in speech and be better communicated.

This was a very educated experience. I was able to help those less unfortunate than me.

Criticisms of s.a.t. test are to highly stress. Just because you don't do good on your s.a.t. doens't mean your going to flunk out of school. Some people just don't test well. Therefor thier abilitys aren't shown to the potential that they are.

I don't like people making fun of me and making me look studip.

References

Mischel, W. (1977). The interaction of person and situation. In D. Magnusson & N. S. Endler (Eds.), *Personality at the crossroads: Current issues in international psychology.* Hillsdale, NJ: Erlbaum.

Vaughan, E. D. (1977). Misconceptions about psychology among introductory psychology students. *Teaching of Psychology, 4,* 138–140.

6
Experimental Psychology

Informed Consent
With Rattus Norvegicus:
Issues, Challenges, and Tidbits

Anthony P. Thompson, Ph.D., Jeanette Thompson, and Al Bino

Training, Research, and Professional Studies
(TRAPS) Institute

Informed consent is one of the ethical cornerstones upon which experimental and clinical psychology rest. Although the psychological community continues to refine its understanding of consent issues, particularly with regard to special populations (e.g., children and the mentally ill), not a squeak has been heard about these matters as they apply to Rattus Norvegicus. Researchers are faced with formidable, but not insurmountable, problems in addressing "informed consent" with this vulnerable, ever-multiplying population.

The three prongs of valid consent are competency, voluntariness, and information. Thus, consent needs to be the informed and voluntary decision of a subject who has the capacity to weigh options. Some have argued that certain classes of subjects have diminished capacity to reason and make choices, a position that has relied almost exclusively upon research designed to assess verbal reasoning skills. However, nonverbal or performance-based measures of problem solving yield different results. For example, a series of our own studies (Thompson & Shrew, 1987; Thompson, Shrew, & Shrew, 1988; Thompson, Shrew, Shrew, & Shrew, 1989) showed conclusively that on the performance measure of the Wexler Intelligence Scale Kit-Rodent (WISK-R) (Wexler, 1987), particularly the mazes sub-test, Rattus Norvegicus adults demonstrated an impressive ability to reason and problem solve. Thus, we assert that healthy adult rats should not be denied the right to make choices simply because of inferior verbal skills as these are adequately compensated for by superior performance abilities.

Voluntary decisions are those not made under undue influence or duress. Concerns have been expressed about the legitimacy of consent when captive populations, including prisoners and introductory psychology students, participate in research endeavors. The agreement of such subjects is likely to be influenced by subtle pressures or contingencies. We note the disturbing trend of most experimental rats being drawn from captive populations. It is unlikely that voluntary consent can be obtained from incarcerated rat subjects. Moreover, we deplore the common practice of offering insidious inducements, such as food and saccharine solutions, in exchange for research participation. Some bold initiatives by Ratfink (1992) at Rottnest Free University have suggested a participation protocol that virtually ensures voluntary participation. Inspired by Pinel's unshackling of inmates at L'Hôpital Saltpétrière, Dr. Ratfink sprung the cage doors on the entire Rattus Norvegicus experimental colony. Although few actually remained in their cages, Ratfink's procedure is still appealing in its simplicity for obtaining truly voluntary research participants. In response to the criticism that this protocol makes it difficult to conduct research with sizable samples, Ratfink is quick to point out that truly voluntary rats exhibit a much higher motivational level than their coerced counterparts. Ratfink's work confirms a much earlier field trial (Piper, 1650) in which nonincarcerated rats in the town of Hamelin were found to readily enlist in an experimental migration project.

Experimental subjects should be provided with information about the purpose of the research and the risks and benefits of participation. They should also be given appropriate guarantees of anonymity or confidentiality. This information is usually outlined in an introductory letter, and increasingly subjects are being asked to provide their signature on a consent form to confirm agreement. Researchers have too hastily dismissed this procedure for Rattus Norvegicus. In our own laboratories, rats to whom we gave written explanations of the research (admittedly simple and brief), were, given ample time, able to digest the content completely. These animals expended considerable energy taking in every shred of information, and they clearly enjoyed the opportunity we afforded them. However, not all the news was good from these initial trials. There was a determined and unanimouse unwillingness to provide written consent. In fact, subjects chewed the pens and defiled the consent forms. The strength of this protest suggested that our protocol had overlooked a basic right.

It was the offhanded comment of a graduate student that helped reveal the problem. Frustrated by hours of searching for his particular animal subject in our emancipated colony, his lips and fingers bruised from ceaseless pipe playing, the student was heard to remark, "These dirty rats all look the same!" Naturally, we were appalled by this racist perspective, and we could not let it go at that. There was more to the tale. To dismantle the barriers of stereotyping, we pointed out to our junior colleague the distinctive and endearing features of each animal. In a flash, we realized why signed consent had been resisted. We had given no assurances of anonymity for Rattus Norvegicus participating in research. We are pleased to report that a local manufacturer has been assigned a contract to produce masks for our research animals to preserve their anonymity. We are hopeful that this safeguard will result in many more signed consent forms and hence remove the final impediment to competent, voluntary, and informed consent by Rattus Norvegicus.

References

Pipe, P. (1650). *Catchy tunes for roving rodents: Preliminary report to the Hamelin town council* (Report No. 1650-1). Brussels, Belgium: Author.

Ratfink, U. (1992). *The liberated animal.* New York: Rottnest Free Press.

Thompson, A., & Shrew, A. (1987). WISK-R administration skills: Cross-species training. *Journal of Rodent Assessment, 3,* 12–17.

Thompson, A., Shrew, A., & Shrew, A., Jr. (1988). WISK-R administration skills: Transfer of training across generations. *Inheritance: A Journal of Inherent Interest, 15,* 123–129.

Thompson, J., Shrew, A., Shrew, A., Jr., & Shrew, A., III. (1989). WISK-R performance IQs: Normative data for Rattus Norvegicus. In U. Neek (Ed.), *Norms for special populations* (pp. 10–12). Thunder Bay, ON: Bar Press.

Wexler, T. (1987). *Wexler Intelligence Scale Kit-Rodent.* Toronto: The Psychillogical Corporation.

A Psychological Study of Things

Seymour Allbright, ABD[1]
Hempstead Community College

The aim of this research was to study some incredibly interesting psychological issues. Specifically, I wanted to learn about how people, men and women, think, talk, and feel about things. What things? Lots of things, all kinds of things.

There have been absolutely no studies of this kind reported in the literature. I know because I used Psych Lit and typed in "things" and found no references at all. None. I was pretty amazed. So there's a tremendous need for this kind of study.

Following are some of the hypotheses and research questions I thought about:

1. How do people think and feel about the things that they think and feel about?

2. Why do people think about these things?

3. Are there any differences? How come?

---

[1] All But Doctorate. Professor Allbright is an untenured assistant professor in the Department of Psychology at Hempstead Community College.

Method

Subjects

Lots of subjects were found for the study. Some were men; the rest were women. They came from all over the place. Although only some of them had children of their own, most of them had been children at some point. The mean age of this sample was somewhere between 15 and 70; that's about what the median was too. I'm not sure what the mode was because some of them fell out of my briefcase on my way to the computer center.

Instruments

Just to be careful, I used every measure in the testing file. I used the WAIS, Rorschach, TAT, MMPI, Draw-A-Person, and Millon. I may have used a couple more but I really don't remember. I think some of them may have been missing pieces. Is it the WAIS or the MMPI that comes with dice? I also think some of the scoring manuals may have gotten mixed up in different boxes. But everybody took the same tests, so it probably doesn't make a difference. One thing that may have made a difference though is that I couldn't find a stopwatch. I hope it was O.K. that I counted "One-Mississippi, Two-Mississippi" while they were doing the puzzles. And some of those puzzles are too damn hard, especially when you're missing pieces.

Procedure

Not every person took every test. That would have taken much too long. So, I gave each person the same number of tests (somewhere around five, I think) and told them to do the best they could. Still, some people started complaining and asking questions about what they were supposed to do. When that happened I just repeated, "Do the best you can."

As for informed consent: I asked everyone if it was O.K. with them that I was doing this. Almost everyone said "sure."

Results

Tons of data were scored and the reliability was more than adequate. Maybe even great. I didn't do test-retest reliability because I didn't think I'd be able to find everyone again. Validity was very, very high except for one measure that was just so-so. Besides, according to Steve, he's the stat consultant all the faculty members use and couldn't get their stuff published without him, all the tests had all the kinds of validity that start with the letter "C".

I ran a bunch of tests using a program that I copied from someone and found some interesting results. For example, most of the tests were correlated with each other.

Let's put Table 1 here, O.K.?

Table 1. Correlations and One-way Analysis of Variance

Men	3.875	.678956	.2	.78954	F = 3.45	
Women	1.24	3.21111	16.0	.89	.34	F = 6 (or maybe 8)
Other	.45	.45	.45	.45	.45	

As Table 1 clearly shows, there were significant differences among men and women and others, even though most of the tests seem to be different from each other.

Discussion

This study was about whether men and women are different on their gender. As you can see—and I expect you to look at the table now, O.K.?—the results are really incredible. The numbers show that "other" was much more consistent than men or women in the way they think and feel (though it's also possible that this might have something to do with the fact that I spilled some soda on the computer disk).

Clearly, the ways that men and women think and feel about things is something that psychologists should be thinking about and studying and telling their students about and also their patients and their patients' friends, too, and they should be getting MacArthur genius grants to discover whether there is a biological difference between men and women or whether it's because of cultural diversity issues. This was an important piece of research because, as you can see, the F was significant at the 6 or 8 level. (If the F had gotten to 10, would I have gotten a free game?)

I think there were a few limitations to this study, but, hey, so what? In conclusion, people should continue to think and feel whether they are men or women or other. I recommend future research on this and every other topic.

Barry A. Farber, Ph.D.
Teachers College, Columbia University

7
Developmental Psychology

Pacifying the Inner Child Within

Jane P. Sheldon, Ph.D.

No matter what our age or how mature we may be, we all have within us our Inner Child self—our creative, playful, alive, true self. Unfortunately, our parents and the society in which we live have helped us to deny this True Self by insisting that we become responsible, rational, emotionally stable adults.

How do our parents squelch our Inner Child? Because our parents' Inner Child True Self was denied to them, they use us, their Outer Child, as their own Inner Child in order to satisfy their own needs. Our parents' lack of perfection in parenting can result in the stifling of our Inner Self so that we experience feelings of guilt, overresponsibility, inadequacy, confusion, and blame.

To rid ourselves of these problematic feelings and pacify our Inner Child Within, we must embark on a path of recovery. We must learn to experience fully our feelings and stop simply doing what others tell us to do. By experiencing, identifying, and talking about our feelings, we can transform, restructure, redefine, and transcend.

The best way to progress is to work on a single issue. For instance, if a person chooses a career in which she devotes her life to helping others, her own needs may then go unmet. Her overdeveloped sense of responsibility may keep her in denial of her Real Inner Child. On the other hand, if she is able to find a way to express her anger and frustration to others, she then may be able to experience the full range of emotion (such as disgust, anger, resentment, and hatred for the idiots who are *unable to solve their own stupid problems without her having* to explain every obvious, simple fact to them). tHis expreshun will then reZult in a tranzfermashun -- a discovree of her own needz zo that ehe can Fiud HEr trEw iuuEr cHtil

On Identity: A Historical Perspective on "Who Am I"

Kenn Finstuen, Ph.D.
U.S. Army—Baylor University

Identity Concept	Source	Date
"Huh?"	Og, Neanderthal caveman	circa 10000 B.C.E.[1]
"Gnothe se auton" (Know thyself)	Oracle at Delphi, Greek	2000 B.C.E.
"I am that I am"	God to Moses in *Exodus*	1250 B.C.E.
"All is nothing, I am all"	Swami Vishnihushi, Sanskrit	1000 B.C.E.
"Nosce te ipsum" (Know thyself)	Virgil, inscription at the shrine of the Vestal Virgins, Rome	50 B.C.E.
"I am the way, the truth, and the life"	Jesus Christ, Hebrew	30 A.D.
"To be or not to be, that is the question"	William Shakespeare	1600
"Cogito ergo sum" (I think therefore I am)	René Descartes, French philosopher	1640

(*continued*)

Identity Concept	Source	Date
"To be is to do" (Essence precedes existence, the categorical imperative)	Immanuel Kant, German philosopher	1780
"Ne te quisiverus extra" (Do not search outside of yourself)	Ralph Waldo Emerson, American essayist	1870
"Anatomy is destiny"	Sigmund Freud, Austrian psychoanalyst	1920
"To do is to be" (Existence precedes essence)	Jean Paul Sartre, French philosopher	1935
"I yam what I yam"	Popeye the Sailor, American	1942
"Do be do be do"	Frank Sinatra, American	1954
"I didn't do it"	Richard Milhous Nixon, American	1974
"Huh?"	Kato Kaelin, O.J. Simpson trial	1995

[1] B.C.E. = Before the Christian Era (a politically correct approach to measuring time)

8
Statistics

On the Application of Clinical Psychology to Statistics: A Psychodiagnostic Case Study of "the Standard Deviation"

Charles G. Middlestead, M.A.
University of Maryland

Once upon a time there was a family of statisticians called the Numburrs. They lived in an upper middle-class community, a safe town, where there was a low crime rate and small deviations. Eigen, the father, was known for being robust, and Alpha, the mother, was known for her significance in the community. Eigen and Alpha had two children: the daughter was named Anova and her brother was Chi. Eigen valued the trust and responsibility that he had worked hard to develop in his two children. But there were problems, the children were discovering sex. Anova was traditional, whereas her brother was developing homogeneity of regression tendencies. This had Eigen and Alpha attenuated.

Both parents had preplanned the birth of Anova, who was the older child. Chi was another story. Chi's birth was most unexpected. Alpha had taken the Bonferroni test along with birth control pills to reduce Familywise Type I Error, but somehow this all failed and Chi was born. Now that he was a teen, he was proving to be quite a test for independence.

Recently, Alpha walked into Chi's room, and discovered him manipulating his variables with a covariate buddy of his, Rho. Instantly, thoughts of autocorrelation and F ratios popped into her mind and she knew that Chi was going to be trouble now that he was able to test his own significance.

When Eigen came home that evening, Alpha intercepted him and they both sloped to the living room to discuss their problematic son.

To their horror, Anova was with her new boyfriend, Gamma, lying on the sofa, and engaged in goodness-of-fit, pair-wise contrasts, and multiple regressions. Alpha shrieked, "Anova has a sex dummy in my living room!" Eigen grabbed Gamma by his decimals and threw him out of the house. With Gamma factored out of the equation, the two badly shaken parents collected their over-sexed children and brought them into the kitchen for a family meeting.

Eigen said, "Children, I always thought that we as a family were part of a normal distribution. You children have high degrees of freedom . . . not to mention hormones. You both are grounded from all forms of sex until you are 21.68 years old . . . make that 22, I forgot to round up."

Anova contorted leptokurtically and whined, "But Pops, why should I get grounded just because Chi is square? If his cell size wasn't so small, he wouldn't be interested in other guys' contingency tables! Besides, Gamma and I are computed from the same sample . . . we're in looooove."

Chi jumped in, "Hey, wait just a point-interval Sis! I ain't square, I'm just as robust and orthogonal as Dad, I just have a different standard deviation, that's all."

Anova grinned devilishly, "Yes . . . significantly, you'll always be a sum of squares."

Just as Chi was getting ready to adjust his sister's Y-axis, Alpha cried, "Look at yourselves, see how you interact—you're both mean squares! Where's your pride, where's your sibling love, where are your critical values?"

The children paused, reflecting on their mother's iterations. They then went over and hugged their parents parsimoniously. They proclaimed, "Mom and Dad, we're done with sex, we want to minimize our error terms and maximize our power!" Eigen looked at his wife and said, "Honey, I believe their claims to be valid and reliable." Alpha beamed, "Yes, our little ones have seen the light. . . . Chi will start having straight relationships, and Anova will stop having linear ones!"

With that, they all held hands, formed a Cramer's V, and lived happily ever after . . . well at least for the product-moment.

9
Contemporary Issues in Psychology

The Americans With Disabilities Act and Its Impact on "Vitally Impaired Persons": Accommodating the Non-Living

David A. Bownas, Ph.D.

The Americans with Disabilities Act of 1990 (ADA) requires that employers not discriminate against individuals with disabilities, and that employers make reasonable accommodation for employees and/or applicants who have disabilities. The sole exception is that candidates or employees who are unable to perform the essential functions of a job may be denied employment, even though the inability to perform is related to the disabling condition.

Psychologists have long played a proactive role in affording opportunities for people with disabilities. Our training makes us uniquely able both to evaluate people's aptitudes and abilities and to deal with the special emotional needs of disabled employees, their co-workers, and organizational clients. Furthermore, psychological journals have for years employed blind reviewers to screen articles submitted for publication. The *Journal of Polymorphous Perversity* has taken an especially active role in promoting acceptance of a particularly vulnerable group of Americans: the dead (Budd, 1992; Menahem, 1984; Templeman, 1991).

The ADA raises a number of issues for employers with respect to the dead. First (and perhaps most significant in promoting public awareness of and sensitivity to this condition), the ADA illustrates the symbolic and attitudinal importance of distinguishing between the disability and the person who *has* the disability. Thus, it is tacky to refer to "the dead," to "dead people," or even to the semantically sanitized "biologically impaired." Instead, we should encourage use of the phrases "person with vital deficits" or "Vitally Impaired Person" (VIP). Such language not only emphasizes that dead people are first and foremost people, who only incidentally happen to be postmordant, but also encourages us to think of the entire range of possible points on the life–death continuum: some people have more severe biotic impairments than others. This is the primary issue ADA raises, in part because it focuses directly on changing underlying public attitudes toward the dead, and also because, being purely semantic, it requires little mental effort and no monetary cost.

The second issue to be addressed concerns whether death (impaired vitality) is a disabling condition. At first glance, it seems possible that Congress did not consider it so. The ADA lists a number of specific impairments that qualify as disabilities under the law (e.g., epilepsy, heart disease, or visual, speech, and hearing impairments), but death is conspicuously absent. However, a closer reading clearly indicates submarginal vivacity will be considered a covered disability under the Act.

To so qualify, an individual must have a permanent or temporary physical or mental impairment that substantially limits one or more major life activities; have a record of such an impairment; or be regarded as having such an impairment.

The phrase *physical or mental impairment* means any physiological disorder or condition, cosmetic disfigurement, or anatomical loss affecting one or more body systems.

The phrase *major life activities* means such functions as caring for one's self, performing manual tasks, walking, seeing, hearing, breathing, learning, and working.

The phrase *regarded as having such an impairment* means that the person has a physical impairment that substantially limits major life activities as a result of the attitudes of others toward such impairment.

We must, then, conclude that dead people *do* have a disability.

Some firms may attempt to discriminate against VIPs by claiming that they are unable to perform the essential functions of many jobs. However, this is an unacceptable distinction, as is evidenced by the difficulty in distinguishing between postbiotic workers and normal workers at times other than payday and quitting time. As neither of these situations represents an essential job function, our ability to distinguish the quick from the dead during the remainder of the work week precludes debarring the vitally impaired from the workplace on the basis of their disability. This opens the door for the third issue raised by ADA: reasonable accommodation.

Reasonable Accommodation in Selection Procedures

Individuals with a disabling condition that might impair their performance on a standardized employee selection procedure must be reasonably accommodated in the testing process. Dead people actually seem to be able to accommodate reasonably well to most situations. They settle in, as it were.

But in the case of preemployment testing, the deceased may need some assistance. As VIPs often perform poorly on written tests as a result of their disability (Goldman, 1987), they may require the aid of a reader, an interpreter, or both. Furthermore, because their disability often impairs manual dexterity and flexibility, some assistance in responding to paper-and-pencil tests may also be required. Pilot tests have shown that VIPs perform quite well on multiple-choice tests using mark-sensitive answer sheets if they are assisted in grasping the pencil (which they frequently accomplish with a firmness bordering on rigidity). The facilitator moves the answer sheet beneath the pencil point to darken response options which the VIP would surely select—if it were not for his or her disability.

Submarginal bioticity is not a handicap in employment interviews. Indeed, research has shown that the favorability of evaluations given to interviewees is directly related to the proportion of time the interviewer spends talking (Webster, 1964). In this context, the VIP will win hands-down, especially if he or she is laid out that way.

Reasonable Accommodation on the Job

Once a vitally impaired candidate has been reasonably accommodated around the selection process, the organization is faced with the challenge of developing performance on the job. Here, again, employees must be reasonably accommodated on a case-by-case basis.

The Equal Employment Opportunity Commission, in its regulations implementing the ADA, suggests several strategies for accommodating employees with disabilities. One obvious step is to provide a reader/interpreter for the vitally impaired employee to facilitate communication and information processing. Another approach is to divide tasks among the people in a work group, assigning VIPs those tasks for which they display particular aptitude. In a reception area, for instance, nonimpaired employees can answer phones, greet visitors, and answer inquiries, while postvital workers can prop doors open, hold directional signs, and hide cracks in the wall.

If a VIP is simply unable to perform a job satisfactorily, reasonable accommodation might require the company to reassign him or her to a more suitable position. For instance, in a retail clothing establishment, a postmordant employee who cannot acceptably answer customer inquiries might work out very well as a mannequin. In a furniture showroom, a thanatotic worker can serve the dual functions of illustrating bedding displays and discouraging small children from bouncing on the display units. In a theatrical production, the biotically impaired would more logically be cast as Hamlet's father than as Hamlet. Indeed, VIPs in a more advanced stage of the condition might more appropriately be considered for the role of Yorick, in Act V. It should, by now, be totally unnecessary to point out that the phrase "live theater" is hopelessly insensitive. Vocational opportunities for necrotic employees are limited only by the imagination of the placement specialist.

In summary, the ADA will have a dramatic impact on personnel psychologists. As trained professionals, we must utilize our knowledge and expertise to ensure that every individual is given the opportunity to reach his or her vocational potential. Dealing with people who are vitally impaired is a challenge, but it is hoped that this article makes clear the necessity to do so and, further, that it suggests some practical means of reasonably accommodating the dead in the workplace.

References

Budd, E. C. (1992). Rorschach assessment of the "non-living": Hardly a dead subject. *Journal of Polymorphous Perversity, 9*(1), 12–16.

Goldman, J. J. (1987). On the robustness of psychological test instrumentation: Psychological evaluation of the dead. *Journal of Polymorphous Perversity, 4*(1), 5–11.

Menahem, S. E. (1984). Psychotherapy of the dead. *Journal of Polymorphous Perversity, 1*(1), 3–6.

Templeman, T. L. (1991). A twelve-step program for the dead. *Journal of Polymorphous Perversity, 8*(2), 8–9.

Webster, E. D. (Ed.). (1964). *Decision making in the employment interview.* Montreal: Eagle.

Spartan Life & Casualty

1 Review Way
Normal, IL 61761

Our credo: Freud said denial is a defense mechanism.
We say denial is the goal of our claims review process.

Mental Health Care   TEL.: 800-336-4257
Claims Division   800-DEN-IALS

Dear Mental Health Professional:

We are in receipt of your recent submission of paperwork requesting preauthorization of ___ sessions of individual/group/
marital/family/other therapy for your patient, Mr./Ms. _____.
Your application is presently undergoing our review process, and
you can expect to receive a Notice of Denial of Preauthorization
(or Notice of Acceptance of Preauthorization) from us within the
next 6 to 12 months.

The following case studies are presented in order to help you to
develop a better understanding of our review process and the
rationale behind our decisions regarding the rejection/acceptance
of preauthorization requests, the types of treatments rejected/
accepted, and the limited number of sessions preauthorized. At
first glance, many of the cases here appear to be extremely complex, requiring prolonged courses of psychological treatment rendered by highly skilled and sensitive therapists. However, we believe that too much has been made of what are, in fact, minuscule
problems that can be quite effectively treated by briefer—and
cheaper—therapeutic methods. In short, it is our view that much of
what many clinicians consider the "drama, complexity, grandness,
and mystery of human life" amounts to simple chemical imbal-
ances and bad habits, treatable by medical or educational manage-

146

ment. The treatment approaches that we recommend in each of the following clinical vignettes are merely guidelines and should not be considered mandatory, although, because we developed these guidelines, we will not authorize additional sessions beyond those specified in each case. Any arguments to the effect that the providers are experts in psychotherapy and assessment and have actually *seen* the patients, whereas neither is true of our in-house reviewers, will, as usual, have no bearing on our decision.

Case example: Adam and Eve (no surname given)

Sessions authorized: 4 (Adam); 2 (Eve); 0 (conjoint marital)

Rationale: Therapist presented case of a dysfunctional marital situation, requesting an initial block of 20 individual sessions plus additional sessions for couples counseling. Request for couples sessions is being denied as marital dysfunction is a V-code in the *DSM-IV* (*Diagnostic and Statistical Manual of Mental Disorders, 4th Edition*) and treatment is not medically necessary, even if, as therapist states, this will doom mankind forever to having to claw out a meager living from the dust of the earth and doom women, in particular, to the excruciating pain of childbirth. (We are not *really* in the prevention business, and certainly not prevention of that magnitude!) Ms. Eve did manifest impulsive personality traits and a possible eating disorder (involving cycles of binging and eternal damnation), so two sessions were authorized for additional assessment, with a recommendation for referral to an Appleholics Anonymous group (if other members can be found in her garden area). Mr. Adam was seen as less impaired, in part because he is male, and so the apple incident described in your report was really Eve's fault; he was considered to be somewhat codependent, however, and so four sessions were authorized for treatment of this condition so that he can learn who is supposed to be in charge. In the long run we think they and their progeny will be happier when he does.

Case example: Oedipus

Sessions authorized: 5

Rationale: Several therapists have made much of this man's difficulties, but we frankly don't see what the fuss has been about and we doubt that he truly has problems with a so-called Oedipus complex. We could not decide if he was the victim or perpetrator of sexual abuse with regard to his mother, so no sessions were authorized for that situation. PTSD (Posttraumatic Stress Disorder) symptoms reported after the murder of his father were not significant; in fact, we note that he went on to function successfully as king and husband. Although there was some self-injurious behavior, it amounted to only one episode (blinding himself), so appeals to a possible "borderline" personality did not move us, and blindness is a condition not usually amenable to psychotherapy. Five sessions were allowed to process the various adjustment difficulties he has had and so that he could ponder the question of what walks on four legs in the morning, two in the afternoon, and three in the evening. In a time-limited group format, of course.

Case example: Hamlet, Prince of Denmark

Sessions authorized: 1 (medication management only)

Rationale: To authorize or not to authorize?—that was our question. The patient and his therapist wrote eloquently (in "Act I, Scene 4" per therapist's notes—such an odd way of doing case reports) about the "vicious moles of nature" that undermine people's lives, and certainly he has demonstrated symptoms of either a psychotic depression or great cunning and deviousness in plotting a revenge. (The reviewers were unable to decide between the two.) He does come from a rather dysfunctional family, but as in the cases cited above, we do not consider that to be an automatic justification for extended treatment. We initially considered a recommendation for brief therapy, however upon review of the transcript of the session between him and Messrs. Rosencrantz and Guildenstern (Act III, Scene 2), in which he makes the point that if they can't learn to play a musical instrument in just a few sessions, they are unlikely to be able to learn enough about him to "play on him" in such a short time, we decided that his noncompliance with brief therapy would be too great. One session will be sufficient to get him on some Prozac before something really awful happens; we suggest that it be administered into his ear.

Case example: Faust

Sessions authorized: 0

Rationale: Case of a man worried about the fact that he had sold his eternal soul to the devil. Treatment is being denied based on a lack of data showing statistically significant relationships between selling one's soul and diagnosable psychiatric conditions. In short, we don't think that one automatically has a psychiatric condition just because one has sold one's soul to the devil. Certainly, none of us have had any such problems!

Case example: Twist, Oliver

Sessions authorized: 1

Rationale: While this child has had a few minor adjustment difficulties following some unfortunate psychosocial experiences, we frankly don't think his problems require psychotherapy so much as immersion in long days of backbreaking child labor to teach him to mind his manners—and his elders. He is merely one of the "worried well." Please don't ask for more.

Case example: Ahab, Captain

Sessions authorized: 4 group sessions, no individual

Rationale: Middle-aged sea captain with obsessive behaviors, including polishing wooden leg and relentlessly pursuing a great white whale. We would consider a referral for medication for obsessive behaviors; characterological features are not exactly *not* covered, but we prefer to act as if they aren't, so they aren't. It is noted that his condition has not interfered significantly with his vocational performance; i.e., he still manages to function as captain of a whaling vessel, to command a ship's crew, and to pursue great white whales with the energy and drive that should lead to vocational success and eventually to a peaceful retirement. Several group sessions for PTSD symptoms are approved. In closing, we would like to ask the therapist whether it was necessary to have written such a *long* preauthorization request in this case.

Case example: Dorothy, Scarecrow, Tin Man, Lion, Toto

Sessions authorized: 0

Rationale: This group of four individuals and a little dog is being denied in one paragraph since their reports were submitted together; we concluded that none have conditions requiring medical treatment, and that all of them would be considered prime examples of "worried well" individuals who are constantly in search of some kind of magical solution to their problems.

While the little girl who ran away from her Aunty Em's home *may* have a conduct disorder (after all, she did kill the so-called wicked witch whose assertiveness she found threatening), and there has been one incident of opiate intoxication ("poppies" abuse), we would point out that running away from home, singing and dancing, hanging around peculiar, oddly attired friends with grandiose expectations, experimenting with mood-altering substances, and occasionally indulging a fetish for fancy footwear are all normative among adolescents, just as among psychologists attending out-of-town meetings.

The conditions alleged by Messrs. Scarecrow and Tin Man are not listed in either *DSM-III-R* (*Diagnostic and Statistical Manual of Mental Disorders, 3rd Edition—Revised*) or *DSM-IV*. We would add that the conditions of brainlessness and heartlessness, far from being disabling, can be assets in certain professions, not excluding our own.

As for Mr. Lion's allegation, we acknowledge that his lack of courage does resemble the *DSM-III-R* condition of Avoidant Personality Disorder. However, we are reluctant to fund treatment of Axis II issues. Moreover, in some cases, cowardice can also be an asset. It might be argued that a society functions most smoothly when its citizens lack the courage to question; certainly, a generalized lack of courage among mental health professionals has made *our* job easier.

Finally, we feel that the most cost-effective alternative for the little dog, Toto, is that he be put to sleep.

Gregory Korgeski, Ph.D.

Critical Considerations in Choosing to Become a Psychologist

Joseph J. Palladino, Ph.D.
University of Southern Indiana

Mitchell M. Handelsman, Ph.D.
University of Colorado at Denver

The last decade has been very stressful for psychologists; research suggests that a high percentage of psychologists, in both academic and applied settings, would train in different fields if they had the choice. Pressures from within and without the discipline have taken much of the pleasure out of a once satisfying field.

Stories about dwindling research money and increasing competition with our colleagues in biology, chemistry, and physics for the shrinking supply of research dollars are all too common. More and more, the public views psychologists as weird people who lie in order to get at the truth, who appear on talk shows, or who do both. In the applied realm, psychologists are in the midst of an era of managed care; anticipated health care reform will diminish practitioners' remunerative opportunities and professional independence. The proliferation of alternative mental health services has prompted psychology to become more adversarial and conservative, with little room left for the innovation and intellectual excitement that has characterized most of our history.

The implication of these trends are potentially grave. A generation of students will be taught by psychologists who are not optimistic about the future of the field, and these students will not graduate with the spark that is necessary for an intellectual rebirth. Mental health services will suffer without the conceptual rigor and high fees that psychology has claimed for so many years. Moreover, social hours at conventions will become deadly serious. Therefore, as a first step to rebuilding the morale within our profession, we here delineate a multitude of reasons to actually be proud of being psychologists. Through exhaustive research, we have developed a list that is designed to cover a broad range of psychological activities.

Reasons We're Proud to Be Psychologists

We know the correct answers to all items on intelligence tests.

Our white lab coats stay clean for decades.

Over 200 *DSM-IV (Diagnostic and Statistical Manual of Mental Disorders, Fourth Edition)* diagnoses make for great cocktail hour small talk.

The cornerstones of our science are drooling dogs, people squinting at different-length lines, and the recall of nonsense syllables.

If we tell a seatmate on an airplane that we are psychologists, we have a friend for life.

The Dr. Joyce Brothers giant balloon in the Macy's Day Parade was so lifelike.

Our introductory texts have 76% more boxes than all other disciplines combined.

Rat-food pellets make great mid-afternoon snacks.

Biologists don't have their own radio shows.

Psychologists are second only to exotic dancers in number of appearances on Oprah, Sally, and Donahue.

Most people believe we can read minds.

We knew they would say that.

A Living Will for Mental Health Professionals

Ernst von Krankman, Ph.D.

To: My Family, My Lawyer, My Friends, My Training Analyst, and All Others to Whom It May Concern.

I, _____, being of sound and relatively analyzed mind (after ____ years of __-times-per-week sessions on the analytic couch), do hereby make, publish and declare this to be my Living Will. If the time comes when I can no longer take part in decisions regarding my own future, let this statement stand as an expression of my wishes and directions while I am still of sound mind.

Should I suddenly take an unexplained turn for the worse, before any drastic or irreversible decisions are made, it is my desire that my membershp in the (American Psychological Association, American Psychiatric Association, National Association of Social Workers) be cancelled and the prorated balance of the exorbitant annual membership dues be returned to me.

Ditto for my malpractice insurance premiums.

Should my physician determine that an organ transplant is necessary, it is my expressed wish that, if at all possible, the donor shall be of the same psychoanalytic orientation as myself, and that under no circumstances should the donor be a Kleinian (Melanie, not Robert).

155

Should colleagues from the university psychology department visit me and attempt to elevate my mood at a time when I am incapacitated or in a coma, the following verbalizations from said colleagues shall be expressly prohibited:

> "Sure your present condition is unfortunate, perhaps it's even bad, but where's the evidence that it's *awful?*"

> "Remember: The sun always rises."

However, the following verbalizations are permissible:

> "You know, your condition does appear to be *awfully* bad."

> "I guess the sun also always sets."

No matter what my medical condition, at no time shall I be subjected to visitors while dressed in a gown with a slit up the middle of the back.

If, after reasonable medical intervention, it becomes apparent that I will not be able to resume my private practice, it is my expressed wish that the majority of my patients be referred to my dear friends, as well as able therapists, _____, _____, and _____. Further, it is my wish that all of my difficult-to-treat borderline patients be referred to my obnoxious, know-it-all, may-(s)he-rot-in-hell colleague, _____; may these patients drive you crazy.

It is my wish that, if confined to a hospital, my room be equipped with both a color television and a black-and-white television, so that I may watch colorized movies in their original black and white.

If after a second medical opinion it should be determined that the probability of my continuing to live longer than one billable cycle of my credit card is greater than 50-50, it is my wish that my hospital bill and all related medical bills be charged to my Citibank

American Airlines AAdvantage® credit card so that I can build up my frequent flier miles.

Under no circumstance may a visitor bearing a gift of a copy of one of Jonathan Kellerman's books be permitted to enter my room.

Should there be a need for me to be hospitalized and, after consultation with other hospital specialists, should my treating physician determine that I will not live out the week, then a second container of vanilla ice cream on my dinner tray would be nice.

This statement is made after careful consideration and is in accordance with my convictions and beliefs. It is my desire that the wishes and directions here expressed be carried out to the extent permitted by law.

In Witness Whereof, I have hereunto set my hand and seal to this, my living will, on the _____ day of _____ 19_____.

_____
Signature

_____
Witness

_____
Witness

Just for the Health of It

Richard Lederer

Doctors are generally very smart people. I know because, over the years, some of the most articulate and knowledgeable letters about language that I have received are from members of the medical profession.

But doctors sometimes find it as hard as anyone else to say what they mean. Like everyone else, doctors can occasionally be tongue-depressing, even when they are describing cases.

The tradition of medical mutilation of the English language goes back hundreds of years. Research into early nineteenth-century Missouri death records has produced some curious medical reports; among the causes of death listed were:

- Went to bed feeling well, woke up dead.

- Died suddenly, nothing serious.

- Cause of death unknown; had never been fatally ill before.

- Don't know; died without the aid of a physician.

- Death caused by blow on the head with an ax. Contributory cause, another man's wife.

Here is an off-the-charts lineup of more recent medical fluffs and flubs as actually dictated by doctors around the world. To my

158

knowledge, each nugget in this varicose vein of anguished English has in no way been doctored. Fortunately for the rest of us, unless we happen to be one of the patients, these classics in the annals of curative history have been saved for posterity by medical transcriptionists, who apparently love to have a little fun while taking their jobs seriously:

- The left leg became numb at times and she walked it off.

- By the time he was admitted, his rapid heart had stopped, and he was feeling better.

- Patient has chest pain if she lies on her left side for over a year.

- Prior to the patient's birth, she was informed at all times that her pregnancy was a normal one.

- The patient states there is a burning pain in his penis which goes to his feet.

- Both the patient and the nurse herself reported passing flatus.

- His daughter was given a genealogical examination at the hospital.

- On the second day the knee was better and on the third day it had completely disappeared.

- She has had no rigors or shaking chills, but her husband states she was very hot in bed last night.

- This patient has been under many psychiatrists in the past.

- The patient has been depressed ever since she began seeing me in 1983.

The pelvic examination will be done later on the floor.

- The patient has never been pregnant and denies any reason for this.

- She was divorced last April. No other serious illness.

- The patient was admitted with abdominal pain from the emergency room.

- He was found lying on the bathroom floor by his wife.

- Patient was seen in consultation by Dr. Blank, who felt we should sit tight on the abdomen and I agreed.

- Patient stated that if she would lie down, within 2–3 minutes something would come across her abdomen and knock her up.

- Preoperative diagnosis: herniated dick.

- I will be happy to go into her GI system; she seems ready and anxious.

- Patient was released to outpatient department without dressing.

- I have suggested that he loosen his pants before standing, and then, when he stands with the help of his wife, they should fall to the floor.

- Patient had bilateral varicosities below her legs.

- The patient is tearful and crying constantly. She also appears to be depressed.

- Dr. Blank is watching his prostate.

- Sister Anna Maria is a Catholic nun who is currently in between missionaries.

- The patient was advised not to go around exposing himself to other people.

- Rectal exam is deferred because patient is sitting upright.

- The patient was somewhat agitated and had to be encouraged to feed and eat himself.

- Discharge status: Alive but without permission.

- The patient will need disposition, and therefore we will get Dr. Blank to dispose of him.

- Coming from Detroit, Michigan, this man has no children.

- Patient was admitted and suffered severe pain by Dr. Blank.

- Healthy appearing decrepit 69-year-old white female, mentally alert but forgetful.

- When you pin him down, he has some slowing of the stream.

- Dr. Blank will dictate on the right breast later.

- The infant was handed to the pediatrician, who cried spontaneously.

- The patient was found to have twelve children by Dr. Blank.

- Many years ago the patient had frostbite of the right shoe.

- The patient is a 74-year-old white female who was brought to the ER by paramedics acutely short of breath.

- After his release from Coronary Care, Dr. Blank worked him over.

- The patient developed a puffy right eye, which was felt to be caused by an insect bite by an ophthalmologist.

- The patient refused an autopsy.

- The patient has no past history of suicides.

- The patient expired on the floor uneventfully.

- Patient left his white blood cells at another hospital.

- Apparently the mother resented the fact that she was born in her forties.

- Patient was becoming more demented with urinary frequency.

- Physician has been following the patient's breast for six years.

- This unfortunate 45-year-old woman has known me for about eight years.

- The patient is a 79-year-old widow who no longer lives with her husband.

- The patient's past medical history has been remarkably insignificant with only a 40-pound weight gain in the past three days.

- The right front side of her car was broadsided while the patient was in the passenger seat going through the intersection.

- The patient is a smoker so will be admitted to a smoking bed.

- The nursing home where the patient lives was noted to sputter, cough, and run a fever.

- The bugs that grew out of her urine were cultured in the ER and are not available. I WILL FIND THEM!!!

- He had a left-toe amputation one month ago. He also had a left-knee amputation last year.

- The patient is a 71-year-old female who fractured her little finger while beating up a cake.

- She slipped on the ice and apparently her legs went in separate directions in early December.

- The patient left the hospital feeling much better except for her original complaints.

- The operative field appeared in good condition, with no bleeding, and therefore the patient was terminated.

- The patient experienced sudden onset of severe shortness of breath with a picture of acute pulmonary edema at home while having sex which gradually deteriorated in the emergency room.

Bless the medical transcriptionists who have preserved these boners and boo-boos as a benefit to the health of all of us. May their tribe thrive and multiply!

For more medical madness, have a look at *A Bloopered Guide to Medical Terminology:*

Abdominal. Terrible.

Anatomy. Part of a moleculey.

Appendix. End of a book.

Artery. The study of fine paintings.

Atrophy. A prize.

Bacteria. Inconveniently located room for serving food.

Barium. What you do when CPR fails.

Benign. What you do after you be eight.

Bowel. A letter like *a, e, i, o,* or *u.*

Capillary. What comes before a butterfly.

CAT scan. Searching for kitty.

Cauterize. Made eye contact with her.

Cesarean section. A district in Rome.

Chiropractor. Egyptian doctor.

Coma. A punctuation mark.

Congenital. Friendly.

Enema. Opposite of a friend.

Esophagus. Egyptian burial casket.

Fester. Quicker.

Fibula. A small lie.

G.I. series. Baseball game between teams of soldiers.

Hangnail. A coat hook.

Hemoglobin. Half the world.

Intestine. Without a will.

Kidney. Young person's leg joint.

Lumbar. Wood.

Mammography. Biography about a southern mother.

Medical staff. A doctor's cane.

Minor operation. Coal digging.

Morbid. A higher offer.

Nitrate. Lower than the day rate.

Organic. Church musician.

Outpatient. A person who has fainted.

Pedicure. Bicycle repair.

Postoperative. A letter carrier.

Prostate. For government.

Protein. In favor of young people.

Pulmonary. Referring to railroad cars.

Recovery room. Place to do upholstery.

Secretion. Hiding something.

Seizure. Roman emperor.

Serology. Study of English knighthood.

Serum. Burn 'em.

Splint. A quick run in Tokyo.

Tablet. A small table.

Terminal illness. Getting sick while waiting for the bus.

Tourniquet. Tennis competition.

Tumor. An extra pair.

Urine. Opposite of "You're out."

Varicose veins. Veins that are close together.

Vertigo. What a tour guidebook tells you.

Vitamin. What to do with guests who come to your house.

X ray. A suggestive ray, X-rated.

Sometimes No Heads Are Better Than One: Decapitated Programs for Mental Health Service Delivery

**Brett N. Steenbarger, Ph.D., and
Roger P. Greenberg, Ph.D.**
SUNY Health Science Center at Syracuse

Recent concerns over cost containment in health care have led to considerable interest in capitated programs of mental health service delivery. Such programs deliver a defined package of services for a fixed dollar amount. However, this has generated significant concern among practitioners, who worry that capitated delivery models may not adequately address the needs of the severely mentally ill. Accordingly, there is now a move toward decapitation in the provision of mental health services.

Getting Ahead by Getting a Head: The Decapitation Trend

Unlike capitation, which sets limits on the dollar amounts allotted to treatment per patient, decapitation is a procedure resulting in the removal of the patient's head. While this may, on the face of it, appear to be a novel and radical form of cost containment, it finds ample historical precedent in the traditions of psychosurgery and insulin–coma therapy. Indeed, before the popularization of talk therapy, trephining, or the drilling of holes into the skull, was a common treatment for mental illness, which allowed offending evil spirits to vacate the sufferer's brain. Later, psychopharmacology emerged as a nonsurgical form of decapitation, proving surprisingly effective in the cessation of untoward mental activity.

Although these early forms of decapitation found initial enthusiasm among practitioners, it quickly became apparent that they had limited cost-containment potential. Specifically, the side effects associated with psychosurgery, trephining, and pharmacologic intervention tended to increase rather than decrease subsequent medical utilization.

Under a decapitated health care plan, patients are advised to keep their heads on straight or risk losing them altogether. Interestingly, this dovetails with some of the methods of brief psychoanalytic psychotherapy, which "hock away at the patient's head" (Habib, Dave, & Lew, 1993). In a prospective study of 8,000 patients enrolled in a large city health maintenance organization, actual decapitation needed to be performed only 16 times, with the vast majority of patients indicating that a single cautionary visit was ample treatment (Krueger, 1992). Relapse was nonexistent among the 16 treated individuals; none found the need to return to treatment.

Resistance to Decapitation Procedures

Ethical objections to decapitation still remain, particularly among nondirective practitioners who prefer client-centered forms of cranial displacement. In an intriguing and promising variant, clients are provided with their own medical tools and anesthesia following prolonged exposure to the music of Barry Manilow ("Suture-self, a self-help program of neurosurgery," *Time,* April 1, 1993). Results are roughly comparable to those of traditional decapitation, though some have claimed that nonspecific music effects, rather than the surgical procedure, are responsible for the observed decrease in subsequent medical utilization.

A more significant source of resistance to decapitation comes from the public, especially those in the hat trade. According to some consumer advocates, widespread adoption of a decapitation scheme could result in the loss of millions of dollars to the hair care and cosmetic industries. Further, it could invalidate the painstakingly collected norms of the Wechsler Intelligence Scales. Traditional psychotherapists have also voiced concerns over decapitation, claiming that it would impair the functioning of some (though not all) of their patients.

A very different source of criticism has come from the counseling profession, which faults "medical model" specialties for their "after-the-fact" approach to decapitation (Steenbarger, 1991). Differentiating primary, secondary, and tertiary models of decapitation, counselors have reported success with the proactive use of decapitation as a means of reducing the incidence of such resource-consuming problems as major depression, schizophrenia, and *acne vulgaris.*

The Effectiveness of Decapitation

At present, a number of multisite studies are comparing decapitation with other forms of treatment as a means of limiting health care related costs. In one study, subjects placed in a unique placebo condition in which they were led to believe that their heads had been removed (although they actually remained intact) incurred significant declines in future health expenditures ("I went to a shrink and came out headless," *National Enquirer,* April 1, 1992). An unfortunate side effect, however, was the putatively decerebrated subjects' fixed delusion that they were now chairs of university departments. More recently, Fisher (1993) criticized the above study for its lack of a truly active placebo condition. His study, featuring the use of virtual-reality helmets, apparently was more convincing in its placebo effect, causing patients to actively declare themselves as nominees for the United States Vice-Presidency.

An unusually creative meta-analysis was conducted by Greenberg (1992), who followed the health care utilization of decapitated victims of automobile accidents, serial killers, and automatic seat belts. Greenberg argued that such "naturally occurring" decapitation could not be subjected to placebo effects and hence could serve as an accurate basis for determining cost containment. Consistent with his hypothesis, Greenberg found that the victims' use of medical and mental health services were significantly curtailed following their accidents.

More recently, Greenberg and Steenbarger (1993) have been investigating decapitation as a form of brief therapy, noting that it possesses many of the central ingredients—limited duration, high therapist activity, and focused desired outcome—of traditional short-term modalities.

Decapitation Side Effects

A thorough literature review reveals that decapitation possesses a favorable side effect profile when compared with such other medical treatments as neuroleptics (Antoinette, 1991). Problems with identity diffusion and self-esteem have been noted, as has a sense of loss of stature. Anorexia is on the rise among the decapitated. Domectomy recipients also frequently express concerns about dishevelled hair, an apparent by-product of "phantom-head syndrome." Research is equivocal about whether the beheaded experience increases or decreases in television addiction.

Although some proponents of the procedure acknowledge that "decapitation is not for everyone," most indicate that side effects are short lived and they point to a host of unanticipated benefits for the headless. Narcissistic disorders and trichotillomania become relatively unknown. Similarly, rates of alcohol and tobacco abuse drop and there is a parallel decline in some of the sexual disorders (such as the uncontrollable urge for oral sex).

Nonetheless, the decision to decapitate is not to be taken lightly, as attempts to reverse the procedure have proved problematic. Although Shari Lewis and the Muppet Workshop have provided some intriguing glimpses of future prosthetic possibilities, the greatest success has been achieved with silicone implants. These create a very natural look and feel. However, implant recipients have suffered from a problem with shape constancy, a condition that has come to be known as "beanbag head."

Conclusions

Capitated systems of health care delivery can be viewed as a transitional phase on the way to more promising decapitated alternatives. "Remove the head, free up the bed" has become the rallying cry for a number of health care economists who view decapitation as uniquely poised to halt the alarming rise in health care costs. As studies establish the effectiveness and efficiency of decapitated systems, it is likely that attention will be given to the removal of other bodily parts as cost-containment incentives (Blacky, 1954), although replacement of traditional decapitation is unlikely, given the recent shortage of university department chairs and Vice-Presidential candidates.

Delusions of References

Antoinette, Marie (1993). The comparative efficacy of decapitation vs. cake in quelling civil disorder: A review. *The French Journal of Revolutionary Ideas, 3,* 26–81.

Blacky, The Dog (1954). Hey, why is that knife poised over my tail and why does it make me so anxious? *Journal of Psychoanalytic Cutlery, 13,* 141–154.

Fisher, Seymour (1993, January). I'm not related to Amy and don't even know Joey Buttafuoco [Letter to the editor]. *American Psychologist, 76,* 282.

Greenberg, Roger (1992). An unusually creative meta-analysis. *Journal of Unusually Creative Meta-analyses, 5,* 54–90.

Greenberg, Roger, & Steenbarger, Brett (1993). Comparing treatments: Light therapy, therapy lite, and some of those California therapies you really want to practice but don't dare. *Journal of Great Tasting, Less Filling Treatments, 45,* 34–45.

Habib, Dave, & Lew (1993). Intensive short-term decapitation of your cylinder heads. *Journal of Three Car Guys, 1,* 1.

Krueger, Freddy (1992). Split-half reliability, the cut-off W Rorschach response, and the Necker Cube. *Journal of Overinclusive Theorizing, 13,* 666.

Steenbarger, Brett (1991). Decapitation as a normal life crisis. *Journal of Rose-Colored Conjectures, 19,* 233–800.

NATIONAL UNIVERSITY
LIBRARY   SAN DIEGO

NATIONAL UNIVERSITY
SAN DIEGO
LIBRARY